NATURE GUI

SHENANDOAH
NATIONAL PARK

SHENANDOAH NATIONAL PARK: THE BASICS

History and Facts

Established: December 26, 1935

Visitors: 1,400,000

Designations: Skyline Drive—National Scenic Byway

Natural Historic Landmark: Rapidan Camp; Skyline Drive National Historic Landmark District

National Register of Historic Places: Skyline Drive and Massanutten Lodge plus 11 significant archaeological sites

National Scenic Trail: Appalachian Trail

State: Virginia

Time zone: Eastern Standard Time (EST)

Official park website: www.nps.gov/shen

Physical Features

Acreage: 198,400

Elevation: Lowest point: 535 feet at Front Royal; highest point: 4,051 feet at Hawksbill Summit

Peaks above 3,000 feet: 69

Water resources: 90+ streams; headwaters of South Fork of the Shenandoah River; major contributor to the Rappahannock, James, Potomac Rivers

Wilderness: 79,579 acres (42 percent)

Average annual precipitation: 40 to 60 inches

Temperature range (F): -10°F to 100°F; mean annual temperature near Luray 53.6°F (3 to 6 degrees cooler at higher elevations)

Plant species: 1,400+ species of vascular plants, including 271 species of trees and shrubs; 1,026 herbaceous species, including wildflowers, grasses, and sedges; 55 ferns and fern allies; 359 lichens; 4,476 fungi; 815 non-vascular plants including mosses, liverworts, and hornworts

Animal species: About 200 birds; 53 mammals; 38 fish; 26 reptiles; 24 amphibians, including 1 federally endangered salamander; 72 butterflies; 200+ aquatic insects; and well over 300 invertebrates

Wildlife population estimates: 300 to 800 black bears, 6,000 white-tailed deer

Facilities

All mileages are from north to south. Mile markers in one-mile increments begin at the North Entrance.

Entrance stations: 4—Front Royal (North) Entrance Station at milepost 0.6, Thornton Gap Entrance Station at milepost 31.5, Swift Run Gap Entrance Station at milepost 65.7, Rockfish Gap (South) Entrance Station at milepost 105.4

Visitor centers: 2—Dickey Ridge at milepost 4.6, Harry F. Byrd Sr. Visitor Center at Big Meadows milepost 51.0

Roads: 105 miles of Skyline Drive

Overlooks: 75

Trails: over 500 miles of trails, including 101 miles of the Appalachian Trail

Campgrounds: 5—650 total sites: Mathews Arm at milepost 22.2, Big Meadows at milepost 51.2, Lewis Mountain at milepost 57.5, Loft Mountain at milepost 79.5, Dundo Group Campground at milepost 83.7

Picnic areas: 7—Dickey Ridge at milepost 4.7, Elkwallow at milepost 24.1, Pinnacles at milepost 36.7, Big Meadows at milepost 51.2, Lewis Mountain at milepost 57.5, South River at milepost 62.8, Dundo at milepost 83.7

Lodging: 3—Skyland at mileposts 41.7 and 42.5, Big Meadows at milepost 51.2, Lewis Mountain at milepost 57.5

Food: 4—Elkwallow Wayside at milepost 24.0, Skyland at mileposts 41.7 and 42.5, Big Meadows at milepost 51.2, Loft Mountain at milepost 79.5

NATURE GUIDE TO
SHENANDOAH
NATIONAL PARK

Second Edition

ANN SIMPSON AND ROB SIMPSON

Essex, Connecticut

FALCONGUIDES®

An imprint of Globe Pequot, the trade division of
The Rowman & Littlefield Publishing Group, Inc.
4501 Forbes Blvd., Ste. 200
Lanham, MD 20706
www.rowman.com

Falcon and FalconGuides are registered trademarks and Make Adventure Your Story is a trademark of The Rowman & Littlefield Publishing Group, Inc.

Distributed by NATIONAL BOOK NETWORK

British Library Cataloguing in Publication Information available

Library of Congress Cataloging-in-Publication Data

Names: Simpson, Ann, 1956– author. | Simpson, Rob, 1948– author.
Title: Nature guide to Shenandoah National Park / Ann and Rob Simpson.
Description: Second edition. | Essex, Connecticut : Falcon Guides, an imprint of Globe Pequot, the trade division of The Rowman & Littlefield Publishing Group, Inc., [2023] | Revised edition of: Falcon pocket guide : nature guide to Shenandoah National Park / Ann and Rob Simpson. 2013. | Includes bibliographical references and index.
Identifiers: LCCN 2022060051 (print) | LCCN 2022060052 (ebook) | ISBN 9781493067237 (paperback ; alk. paper) | ISBN 9781493067244 (electronic)
Subjects: LCSH: Natural history—Virginia—Shenandoah National Park—Guidebooks. | Nature study—Virginia—Shenandoah National Park—Guidebooks. | Shenandoah National Park (Va.)—Guidebooks.
Classification: LCC QH105.V8 S58 2023 (print) | LCC QH105.V8 (ebook) | DDC 508.755/9—dc23/eng/20230113
LC record available at https://lccn.loc.gov/2022060051
LC ebook record available at https://lccn.loc.gov/2022060052

♾™ The paper used in this publication meets the minimum requirements of American National Standard for Information Sciences—Permanence of Paper for Printed Library Materials, ANSI/NISO Z39.48-1992.

CONTENTS

CONTENTS

SHENANDOAH NATIONAL PARK: NORTH SECTION

Legend

1. Dickey Ridge/ Fox Hollow Trail
2. Mathews Arm/ Traces Trail
3. Beahms Gap Area
4. Stony Man Trail
5. Limberlost
6. Hawksbill Summit
7. Big Meadows
8. Milam Gap/Mill Prong Trail/Rapidan Camp

Shenandoah National Park
Wilderness Area
Appalachian Trail
Skyline Drive

81
11 Strasburg
340
66
340
Front Royal 55
Front Royal (North) Entrance to Washington, D.C. 72 miles
Front Royal (North) Entrance Station

1 5 miles
604

Dickey Ridge Visitor Center
1,940 ft.

Dickey Hill

Low Gap 1,790 ft.
649 10 miles
630
522

Bentonville 613
Browntown

Mt. Marshall 3,368 ft. 15 miles
Jordan River
The Peak 3,000 ft.

Gimlet Ridge

Hogback Mt. 3,474 ft.
Thornton Gap to Washington, D.C. 80 miles

Mathews Arm
2750 ft. 20 miles
2
622

Elkwallow
25 miles
Washington

Pignut Mt. 2,530 ft.
522

South Fork Shenandoah River
340
654
Three Sisters 2,085 ft.
3 Thornton Gap Entrance Station 2,304 Ft.
Covington River
211 Sperryville
Thornton River

Pass Run
30 miles

Park Headquarters
Tunnel Parking Overlook 2,840 ft.
231
522

211 Luray
Marys Rock
Hazel Mt. 2,880 ft.
Hazel River

Pinnacles 3,350 ft.
35 miles

211
40 miles

Skyland
3,680 ft. Highest point on drive
4 Pinnacle Peak 3,401 ft.
600 707
5
601

BUS 340
Bettys Rock
Old Rag 3,268 ft.

Stanley
45 miles
6
643

Byrd Visitor Center, Big Meadows 3,535 ft.
Spitler Hill
50 miles
Rose River
600
231

670 643 600
Syria

7
Rapidan Camp
Doubletop Mountain
649 Robinson River
Banco
670

8
0   5
Miles

340
Hazeltop 3,812 ft.
Fork Mountain
Tanners Ridge

55 miles

Jeremys Run
Hawksbill Creek
Rush River
Rappahannock River

SHENANDOAH NATIONAL PARK: SOUTH SECTION

Grindstone
Mountain
2,850 ft.

Bluff
Mountain

662

Shenandoah

55 miles

Green
Mountain
2,149 ft.

Bearfence Mountain

615

662

759

Lewis Mountain

Lewis
Mountain

606

Kirtley
Mountain
2593ft

665

759

606

607

Piney Mountain
1,975 ft.

60 miles

N
W   E
S

625

9

South
River

0   5

Miles

759

Huckleberry
Mountain
2,158 ft.

623

Conway River

Elkton

624

South River

622

65 miles

Saddleback
Mountain
3,375 ft.

230

33

Swift Run Gap
Entrance Station

340

Hightop
3,587 ft.

McGaheysville

Stanardsville

649

70 miles

33

Swift Run Gap
to Harrisonburg
21 miles

Rocky Mount
2,740 ft.

810

Swift Run

Flattop Mt.
3,320 ft.

Simmons Gap

75 miles

Brown
Mt.

Pinefield Gap 2,530 ft.

Brokenback
Mountain
1,750 ft.

Lynch River

Port Republic

Loft
Mountain

County Line
Mountain
1,980 ft.

659

80 miles

10

Loft Mountain

South Fork Rivanna River

663

Grottoes

Madison Run

Big Flat
Mountain

664

Dundo

810

2520 ft Blackrock
Summit Parking

11

Trayfoot
Mountain
3,374 ft.

85 miles

Blackrock

340

90 miles

614

Bucks Elbow
Mountain
2,787 ft.

Turk
Mountain
2981ft

95 miles

810

250

Charlottesville

619

611

Crozet

Lickinghole Creek

64

29

12

100 miles

Waynesboro

64

Scott Mt.
2,760 ft.

Rockfish Gap
to Staunton
18 miles   105 miles

250

Rockfish Gap (South) Entrance Station

START OF BLUE RIDGE PARKWAY (MILE 105.4)

Legend

9 South River Falls

10 Loft Mountain Area

11 Blackrock Summit

12 Beagle Gap

Shenandoah
National Park

Wilderness Area

Appalachian Trail

Skyline Drive

ACKNOWLEDGMENTS

Many thanks to the superb park personnel and volunteers of Shenandoah National Park who have dedicated their lives to preserving the natural resources of the park and sharing the natural wonders of the park with visitors. We would especially like to thank Mara Meisel, Wendy Cass, Claire Comer, and Park Resource Management and Interpretation staff for sharing their wealth of knowledge about the park's natural history. Our thanks also to Greta Miller and the staff and members of the Shenandoah National Park Association for their continued support of the interpretation and educational mission of the park. We would also like to thank all the staff at Rowman & Littlefield, especially David Legere, whose support and efforts have continued to make this National Park Nature Guide series a reality. Thanks also to Terry Leight for his natural history observations and contributions. We would like to dedicate this book to our family, including our children and their spouses, Jeremiah, Mitzi, Jessie, Jamie, and Aaron, for their love and support. We especially dedicate this book to our precious grandchildren, Georgia, Gracie, Jacob, and Natalie, who constantly remind us about the wonders of the natural world. A moment spent sharing nature with a child is an investment in the future of our world.

To the reader, we hope this guide helps you enjoy the amazing wonders of nature and in doing so generates a spark of love for the plants and animals that rely on us for their continued existence in important natural habitats such as those in Shenandoah National Park.

Park rangers share their knowledge of nature with visitors during informative ranger programs.

PARTNERS WITH SHENANDOAH

Shenandoah National Park Association

The Shenandoah National Park Association (SNPA) is a private, non-profit organization whose sole purpose is to provide support to the interpretive and educational activities of Shenandoah National Park. Established in 1950, SNPA provides support through the sales of educational books, maps, DVDs, and other items on the human and natural history of the park. The profits from the sale of these items in the two visitor center park stores and through mail order are used to fund various programs and activities managed by the Interpretive Division of the park.

Membership in SNPA is open to the public and offers the opportunity to personally support the park as well as receive special discounts on purchases from the association's bookstores. SNPA has a large membership base that continues to support the activities of the association and the park. The association also schedules educational resource seminars throughout the year for participants to gain in-depth information on the natural wonders of the park. Popular seminar subjects include trees, birds, wildflowers, butterflies, and mushrooms, as well as seminars on nature photography, fly fishing, and art. For more information about SNPA, and/or to order items from the park stores or register for the seminars, visit the association online at www.snpbooks.org or call (540) 860-5481.

If you plan a visit to Shenandoah, remember to bring along this informative nature guide to help you explore!

Shenandoah National Park Trust

As the official philanthropic partner of the park, the Shenandoah National Park Trust raises funds that help protect wildlife and wild places, preserve historic structures, educate the next generation, support research, and provide extraordinary recreational experiences. For more information, visit www.snptrust.org.

In perfect form, the large white trillium is the emblem of the Shenandoah National Park Association whose efforts support educational funding for the park.

White blazes guide hikers along the Appalachian Trail leading to majestic vistas in Shenandoah.

Potomac Appalachian Trail Club

The Potomac Appalachian Trail Club (PATC) is a non-profit volunteer organization and member club of the Appalachian Trail Conference. The PATC assumes responsibility for cooperative maintenance and visitor services along the Appalachian National Scenic Trail (AT) and many other foot trails and associated facilities in the Shenandoah National Park and in Virginia, Maryland, and Pennsylvania. The PATC and Shenandoah National Park have been jointly involved in the stewardship of trails since the park's establishment in 1936. For more information, visit www.patc.net.

INTRODUCTION

The *Nature Guide to Shenandoah National Park* is an easy-to-use field guide to help visitors identify some of the most common plants, animals, and natural features of the park. Technical terms have been kept to a minimum, and color pictures accompany the descriptions. Perfectly sized to fit easily into a daypack, this compact field guide is filled with interesting information about each organism, including natural history and ethnobotanical notes and other historical remarks. We care for the things we know. Intended as an introduction to nature in Shenandoah National Park, this book will hopefully spark an interest in the natural world and generate further interest in caring for and supporting the environment. You can refer to the References section at the end of this book for more information and resources for in-depth identification purposes.

About Shenandoah National Park

Skyline Drive stretches for 105 miles through the park from Front Royal to Waynesboro, Virginia, allowing easy access to the mountain vistas and trails. The lush Shenandoah Valley lies to the west and the rolling Piedmont to the east. About 101 miles of the famed Appalachian Trail are located within the boundaries of Shenandoah National Park.

Shenandoah National Park (SNP) is divided into three districts. The North District is between Front Royal and US 211 at Thornton Gap, the Central District begins at Thornton Gap and ends at US 33 at Swift Run Gap, and the South District begins at Swift Run Gap and ends at US 250 at Rockfish Gap. A conservation success story, the natural history of Shenandoah is a fantastic blend of resilience and recovery aided by the forethought and perseverance of those who love nature and the wildlife and wild plants that thrive when given the opportunity.

It is highly recommended that you begin your visit with a stop at one of the visitor centers where you can pick up a park map and learn about activities such as the Junior Ranger program and other events. Along the roadway are numbered mileposts that begin with zero at the North Entrance near Front Royal and end at 105 near Waynesboro. There is an entrance fee for Shenandoah National Park; see the park website for current fees at www.nps.gov/shen. The America the Beautiful–National Parks and Federal Recreational Lands Annual Pass is available, as is the Senior Pass for US citizens age 62 or older. Annual SNP passes are available for $55. Permanently disabled citizens are eligible for a free Access Pass, and active-duty military members and dependents are eligible for a free Annual Pass.

Over 100 miles of the world-famous Appalachian Trail wind through Shenandoah.

Volunteers who acquire 250 service hours are eligible for a free Volunteer Pass. It is good to know that 80 percent of the fees collected at Shenandoah are returned to the park for specific projects.

Although the park is open daily, most of the visitor services are only open from late March or early April to early November. You can check road closures by calling the park information line at (540) 999-3500 or on the park website at www.nps.gov/shen. At a maximum speed limit of 35 miles per hour, it takes at least three hours to travel the 105 miles through the park without stopping. Of course, you should allow more travel time so you can leisurely enjoy the scenic beauty of this exquisite land.

Please check the park website for food and lodging availability in the park. During the peak visitor seasons in the summer and especially in October, the three lodges and five campgrounds typically fill early and advance planning is necessary. Food, lodging, fuel, and other services are available at local towns bordering the park including Front Royal, Luray, Harrisonburg, and Waynesboro. See Mileposts of Common Destinations in or near Shenandoah National Park for help with planning your visit. The Shenandoah National Park Association provides carefully selected educational materials to park bookstores to enrich your enjoyment of the park. Please consider joining the association's efforts to support the educational, research, and other conservation efforts of the park.

Mileposts of Common Destinations in or near Shenandoah National Park

Visitor services in Shenandoah National Park typically open in late March and run to early November. Camping reservations for some campgrounds in the park are available at www .recreation.gov or by calling (877) 444-6777; all others are on a first come, first served basis. For lodging at Skyland, Big Meadows, and Lewis Mountain, visit Skyline Drive | Lodging in Shenandoah National Park (goshenandoah.com) or call (877) 847-1919. Cabins may be available for rent through the Potomac Appalachian Trail Club; visit www.patc.net.

Fuel and other services can be found at towns just off Skyline Drive; please note that there may be lengthy distances between fuel stops and plan accordingly. In the park, fuel is available only at Big Meadows, but gas pumps can be unreliable in the winter. Electric vehicle charging stations are available at Skyland and Big Meadows but may be unavailable. You can check current availability at www.nps.gov/shen/planyourvisit/goods-services.htm.

Toilets are located at visitor centers and most picnic areas. Services may not be available in winter, including lodging, campgrounds, and picnic areas. Also, while all park campgrounds have toilets, they are not available to non-campers.

At Front Royal, Virginia, the North Entrance to Shenandoah National Park is only a few hours' drive from Washington, D.C.

Skyline Drive is normally open twenty-four hours a day, but severe weather or other emergencies may necessitate closure at any time. For more information and the current status, check the Shenandoah National Park website at www.nps.gov/shen or call the park's recorded information line at (540) 999-3500. (Note: Cell phones do not work in many areas of the park but service may be available near Dickey Ridge Visitor Center and at some west-facing overlooks.) Free public WiFi is available at Byrd Visitor Center, Big Meadows Lodge, and the Skyland Dining Room.

Do not rely on GPS to navigate Shenandoah National Park, as it can be incorrect. For more information on the park and other national parks, you can download the free National Park Service app through the App Store (apps.apple.com/us/app/national-park -service/id1549226484) and Google Play (play.google.com/store/apps/details?id=gov.nps .mobileapp).

Skyline Drive Mileposts (MP)

0   North Entrance—off US 340 (also called Stonewall Jackson Highway) near Front Royal, Virginia; 21073 Skyline Drive, Front Royal, VA 22630; GPS 38.905729, −78.198624

4.6   Dickey Ridge—Dickey Ridge Visitor Center, bookstore, gifts, backcountry permits, exhibits, toilets, local/credit card/collect-only phone

4.7   Dickey Ridge Picnic Grounds—picnic area, toilets

22.2   Mathews Arm—campground and amphitheater

24.0   Elkwallow Wayside—food, gifts, camping supplies, toilets, pay phone

24.1   Elkwallow Picnic Grounds—picnic area, toilets

31.5   Thornton Gap Entrance—off US 211 East (also called Lee Highway) near Luray, Virginia; GPS 38.660959, −78.320761

31.6   Panorama—toilets

36.7   Pinnacles Picnic Grounds—picnic area, toilets

41.7 and 42.5   Skyland Resort—lodging, food, gifts, horseback riding, amphitheater; (877)-847-1919

51.0   Big Meadows—Byrd Visitor Center, bookstore, gifts, backcountry permits, exhibits, toilets

51.2   Big Meadows Wayside—food, gifts, camping supplies
        Big Meadows Campground—showers, laundry, amphitheater
        Big Meadows Lodge—food, lodging, gifts; (877) 847-1919
        Big Meadows Picnic Grounds—picnic area, amphitheater, toilets
        Big Meadows—meadow trails, wildlife, plants

57.5   Lewis Mountain Cabins and Campstore—lodging, camping supplies; (877) 847-1919
        Lewis Mountain Campground—emergency phone, campground
        Lewis Mountain Picnic Grounds—picnic area, toilets

62.8   South River—picnic area, toilets

65.5   Swift Run Gap Entrance—off US 33 (also called Spotswood Trail); Shenandoah
        National Park Swift Run Gap Entrance Station; GPS 38.357744, −78.545594; pay
        phone available

79.5   Loft Mountain Wayside—food, gifts, emergency phone
        Loft Mountain Campground—campground, campstore, showers, laundry, amphitheater

83.7   Dundo Picnic Grounds—picnic area, toilets
        Dundo Group Campground

105   Rockfish Gap—South Entrance, off US 250 a few miles east of Waynesboro,
        Virginia, at Afton, Virginia; 282 Skyline Drive, Waynesboro, VA 22980;
        GPS 38.033777, −78.85902; emergency phone available

Nearby Natural Areas and Other Destinations off Skyline Drive

From North Entrance at Front Royal

Front Royal—gateway town to the North Entrance to Skyline Drive with lodging, food, fuel,
    hospital, all services, canoe capital of Virginia; accessible via I-66 and US 340. Front
    Royal/Warren County Chamber of Commerce: (540) 635-3185; www.frontroyalchamber
    .com

Skyline Caverns—caverns, anthodites; 10344 Stonewall Jackson Hwy., Front Royal, VA
    22630; (540) 635-4545 or (800) 296-4545; www.skylinecaverns.com

Shenandoah River State Park—camping, hiking, fishing, wildlife, birding; 350 Daughter of
    Stars Dr., Bentonville, VA 22610; off US 340, 8 miles south of Front Royal and 15 miles
    north of Luray; (540) 622-6840; www.dcr.virginia.gov/state_parks/and.shtml

Cedar Creek and Belle Grove National Historic Park—Belle Grove Manor House, Cedar Creek
    battlefield, hiking, birding, ranger programs; NPS Visitor Contact Station, 7712 Main St.,
    Middletown, VA 22645; (540) 869-3051 or (540) 868-9176; www.nps.gov/cebe

Winchester—Frederick County Convention & Visitors Bureau, 1400 S. Pleasant Valley Rd.,
    Winchester, VA 22601; (540) 542-1326 or (877) 871-1326; www.visitwinchesterva.com

Museum of the Shenandoah Valley—American Indian archaeological presentation, gar-
    dens; 901 Amherst St., Winchester, VA 22601; (540) 662-1473, ext. 235 or (888) 556-
    5799; www.themsv.org

Blandy Experimental Farm and State Arboretum of Virginia—gardens, trails, birding; Orland E. White Arboretum, Virginia Native Plant Trail, 400 Blandy Farm Ln., Boyce, VA 22620; (540) 837-1758; http://blandy.virginia.edu

G. Richard Thompson Wildlife Management Area—wildlife viewing, hiking, wildflowers (including trillium), fishing; permit required to get into this area; exit 17 off I-66 at Markham, VA 55 to Linden, north on SR 638 (Freezeland Road); https://dwr.virginia .gov/wma/thompson

George Washington National Forest—wildlife, hiking, fishing, camping, mountain biking; Lee Ranger District, 95 Railroad Ave., Edinburg, VA 22824; (540) 984-4101; North River Ranger District, 401 Oakwood Dr., Harrisonburg, VA 22801; (540) 432-0187 or (866) 904-0240; www.fs.usda.gov/gwj

Seven Bends State Park—day use only, boat launches, picnic areas, hiking. Hollingsworth Access: 2111 S. Hollingsworth Rd. Woodstock, VA 22664, and Lupton Access: 1191 Lupton Rd., Woodstock, VA 22664; (540) 622-6840

Sky Meadows State Park—hiking, fishing, birding, camping; main entrance on SR 710 less than 2 miles south of Paris, Virginia; 11012 Edmonds Ln., Delaplane, VA 20144; (540) 592-3556; www.dcr.virginia.gov/state_parks/sky.shtml

Potomac Appalachian Trail Club—hike club, cabins; (703) 242-0315; or write to PATC, 118 Park St. SE, Vienna, VA 22180; www.patc.net

Appalachian Trail Conservancy—(304) 535-6331; www.appalachiantrail.org

From Thornton Gap Entrance at Luray

Luray, Virginia—lodging, food, fuel, hospital, all services; Luray & Page County Chamber of Commerce, (540) 743-3915; www.visitluraypage.com/chamber

Shenandoah National Park Headquarters—3655 US Hwy. 211 E., Luray, VA 22835; emergency line: (800) 732-0911; information line: (540) 999-3500; www.nps.gov/shen/index.htm

Sperryville, Virginia—lodging, food, fuel; US 211 and US 522; sperryville.com

Old Rag Mountain Trailhead (SNP)—VA 600 near Nethers, Virginia; emergency phone, tickets required; (877) 444-6777; www.nps.gov/shen/planyourvisit/faqs-oldrag.htm

Whiteoak Canyon Boundary Trailhead (SNP)—VA 600 near Syria, Virginia; emergency phone; https://www.nps.gov/shen/planyourvisit/upload/whiteoakcanyon_roadtrail.pdf

Luray Caverns—caverns, museum, garden maze; 9 miles from SNP, 970 US 211 West, Luray, VA 22835 (address for GPS: 101 Cave Hill Rd., Luray, VA 22835); (540) 743-6551; www.luraycaverns.com. Note: Shenandoah National Park Association membership includes a discount to Luray Caverns.

Luray Zoo—privately owned rescue zoo with reptiles, birds, other animals; 1087 US Hwy. 211 W., Luray, VA 22835; (540) 743-4113; lurayzoo.com

From Swift Run Gap Entrance at Elkton/Harrisonburg

Elkton, Virginia—lodging, food, fuel; (540) 298-1951; elktonva.gov

Harrisonburg, Virginia—lodging, food, fuel, hospital, all services; Harrisonburg–Rockingham Chamber of Commerce, (540) 434-3862; www.hrchamber.org

Edith J. Carrier Arboretum and Botanical Gardens—gardens, trails, birding; James Madison University, 780 University Blvd., MSC 3705, Harrisonburg, VA 22807; (540) 568-3194; www.jmu.edu/arboretum

Endless Caverns—caverns, camping; 1800 Endless Caverns Rd., New Market, VA 22844; (540) 896-2283; www.endlesscaverns.com

Shenandoah Caverns—caverns; exit 268 off I-81; 261 Caverns Rd., Quicksburg, VA 22847; (540) 477-3115; www.shenandoahcaverns.com

Rapidan Wildlife Management Area—wildlife viewing, hunting, fishing (permit required), 4WD vehicle recommended; 25 miles west of Culpeper and 30 miles north of Charlottesville; https://dwr.virginia.gov/wma/rapidan

Massanutten Resort—skiing, nature trails, water park, spa, lodging, food, fuel; about 10 miles west of SNP Swift Run Gap Entrance at Elkton, on US 33 W; 1822 Resort Dr., McGaheysville, VA 22840; (540) 289-9441; www.massresort.com

From South Entrance at Rockfish Gap at Afton/Waynesboro

Waynesboro, Virginia—lodging, food, fuel, hospital, all services; 4 miles west on US 250; www.waynesboro.va.us

Blue Ridge Parkway—469-mile parkway from Virginia to North Carolina to Great Smoky Mountains National Park; just south of milepost 105 on Skyline Drive near Waynesboro, VA; www.nps.gov/blri

Wintergreen Resort—lodging, food, fuel, nature center, fishing, hiking, skiing; take US 250 West to VA 151 to SR 664 or from Blue Ridge Parkway, take Reeds Gap exit; Wintergreen Resort, Route 664, Wintergreen, VA 22958 (address for GPS: 39 Mountain Inn Loop, Roseland, VA 22967; 37.914189, -78.943806); (434) 325-2200; www.wintergreenresort.com

Grand Caverns—caverns, hiking, biking; about 15 miles north of Waynesboro and 20 miles south of SNP Swift Run Gap Entrance at Elkton; 5 Grand Caverns Dr., Grottoes, VA 24441; (540) 249-5705; www.grandcaverns.com

Frontier Culture Museum—frontier and pioneer farming exhibits; 1290 Richmond Rd.,
    Staunton, VA 24402; (540) 332-7850; www.frontiermuseum.org
Natural Bridge State Park—National Historic Landmark with natural bridge, caverns, trails,
    butterfly garden, Monacan Indian Living History Exhibit, lodging, food, fuel; about 1
    hour south of Waynesboro; 6477 S. Lee Hwy., Natural Bridge, VA 24578; (540) 291-
    1326; naturalbridgestatepark.org
Natural Bridge Zoo—animal petting and feed areas, elephant rides, zoo, gift shop; 5784 S.
    Lee Hwy., Natural Bridge, VA 24578; (540) 291-2420; https://naturalbridgestatepark
    .org/attractions/natural-bridge-zoo
Virginia Safari Park—drive-through zoo, animal feeding and encounters; 229 Safari Ln.,
    Natural Bridge, VA 24578; (540) 291-3205; www.virginiasafaripark.com
Charlottesville, Virginia–lodging, food, fuel, hospital, all services: www.charlottesville.gov;
    www.cvillechamber.com

Safety Notes

Skyline Drive is uniquely designed to afford motorists spectacular views that follow the natural flow of the mountains. The maximum speed limit is generally 35 miles per hour, but in some areas it drops to 25 miles per hour or less. There are some steep grades and many winding, tight curves—some with very little sight distance—and areas with narrow shoulders; please slow down in these areas. Use caution when you are passing by or pulling out of one of the seventy-five scenic overlooks along the road. Skyline Drive is also a favorite destination for bicyclists and motorcyclists; watch out for them and give them plenty of space. Perhaps the greatest driving distractions are the magnificent views. Allow time to pull over and enjoy the scenery, and be aware that others may be distracted by the views too. Another hazard is wildlife such as bears and deer that may dash onto the road with little or no notice—many animals are killed each year by speeding or inattentive drivers. Fog often envelops the roadway, especially at the higher elevations; please slow down in foggy conditions. Cyclists must have working headlights and taillights during foggy weather and at night. Roads lack shoulders, and cyclists should plan their trips when traffic is light. Avoid Skyline Drive when it is snowy or icy. There is one tunnel on Skyline Drive: Be sure that your RV or trailer can clear Marys Rock Tunnel (just south of Thornton Gap Entrance from US 211) at 12 feet, 8 inches.

Always let someone know your plans when you go for a hike. Dress in layers and carry raingear and plenty of water, as weather conditions can change rapidly. Be aware of fast-moving streams and waterfalls. Falling trees and branches overhead can present hazards.

Often only a few steps from parking areas and Skyline Drive, the Appalachian Trail beckons hikers.

Cautious driving can prevent wildlife accidents along Skyline Drive, which runs the length of Shenandoah National Park.

Prevent dehydration and sunburn, respectively, by drinking plenty of water and applying sunscreen. Do not drink untreated water from springs or streams; the seemingly clean water may harbor parasites including *Giardia lamblia*, which causes severe diarrhea.

Never feed wildlife. Not only is it illegal but it also endangers the welfare of the animal. Stay a safe distance from all wildlife. There are poisonous snakes (timber rattlesnakes and copperheads) in the park; be careful where you place your hands and feet, especially

No matter how tempting, please remember never to feed wildlife.

when climbing on rocks or in shrubby areas. Although there are no grizzly bears here, black bears do reside in the park. Most will avoid you if they hear you coming. If you encounter a bear, make your presence known by talking quietly and slowly back away. If the bear approaches you, make noise by yelling and clapping your hands. When hiking, keep small children by your side or at least within sight—pick them up if you see a bear on or near the trail. Ticks, mosquitoes, and biting insects can be common throughout the park; take precautions such as using insect repellent and tucking your pants into your socks to prevent bites that may result in Lyme disease, Rocky Mountain spotted fever, or other tick-borne illnesses. If you find a tick attached to you, remove it with tweezers or a tissue and clean the bite. See a health care provider if you later become ill. Bees and wasps (primarily yellow jackets) are found in the park. Carry proper first aid equipment if you are allergic to bees. Poison ivy is common along trails—learn to recognize this three-leaved plant. If you come in contact with poison ivy, wash the affected area with soap and cool water.

Please report emergencies such as accidents, uncontrolled fires, or other safety hazards by calling (800) 732-9111. Any references to ethnobotanical or edible uses of plants or fungi in this book are for academic purposes only; many plants and fungi are poisonous or otherwise harmful.

Conservation Note

Please leave wildflowers and other plants where they grow. When hiking, stay on established trails and watch where you put your feet to avoid damaging plants. Especially in cliff areas, avoid trampling plants, as some of them may only be able to exist in these special conditions. Please keep in mind that it is illegal to pick, dig up, or damage any plant. Please report any suspicious activity such as plant poaching to a park ranger. Remember that all natural resources are protected in the park, including the rocks and minerals. Please leave them for others to observe and enjoy.

How to Use This Book

Common and Scientific Name
In an effort to create consistent communication worldwide, each organism has a Latin name—designating genus and species—that is unique to that organism. Common names of families are given with the scientific family name in parentheses. In many cases an organism may have many common names, often varying in locality. In addition, genetic research is rapidly discovering new inherent relationships and associations, and the taxonomic status of many organisms may change with the new information.

Photo Tips
Sharp focus is the key to taking great nature photos. Overcast days offer nice soft lighting for wildflowers and animals. In deep shade, increase the ISO or use a flash. Bright sunny days create harsh shadows, so stand with the sun at your back and point your shadow at the subject. A flash will add detail to the dark shaded areas of the flower or add a speck of light to the eye. Image stabilization capability will help stop camera motion. For more advanced camera systems, shooting close-ups at f16 with a flash will give more depth of field and stop motion. When taking wildflower photos, be careful not to trample other plants. Use a telephoto lens to zoom in on wildlife and be sure to keep the animal's eye in focus. Never approach too closely just to get a picture. If wildlife changes its behavior in your presence, you are too close. It is illegal to use artificial calls to attract wildlife. It is also illegal to touch wildlife in the park. Approaching wildlife can be unsafe. Be respectful of wildlife and remember it is up to each of us to help protect the animals and their habitats.

Suggested Nature Hikes and Wildlife Viewing Areas
We have listed several of our favorite natural areas and hikes in the park. Several trail maps are available free from the park website (nps.gov/shen/planyourvisit/maps.htm). For additional hike details, consult a park topographic map available from Shenandoah National Park Association (SNPA) (snpbooks.org/product-category/maps) or the Potomac Appalachian Trail Club (PATC) (patc.net/PATC/Our_Store/PATC_Maps.aspx). Hiking trail guidebooks such as *Best Easy Day Hikes in Shenandoah National Park* and *Hiking Shenandoah National Park* (FalconGuides) by Bert and Jane Gildart are available from SNPA. To help

Shenandoah supports one of the largest black bear populations in Virginia.

plan your visit, you can download the free National Park Service app through the App Store (apps.apple.com/us/app/national-park-service/id1549226484) and Google Play (play.google .com/store/apps/details?id=gov.nps.mobileapp).

The following areas or trails are suggested for the general public and families who want to see wildlife, wildflowers, and other natural features of Shenandoah National Park. The mileposts (MP) are given from north to south along Skyline Drive. Some of the recommended trails are wheelchair accessible or accessible with assistance. Of course, the wild animals and plants of the park may not always be where expected, so it is a good idea to first stop at a visitor center and check with a park ranger about recent sightings.

Always maintain a safe distance from wildlife and never feed wildlife. Do not pick any wildflowers or remove any natural or cultural objects from the park. Remember, you are more likely to see wild animals during the early morning and evening, when they are more active. To protect wildlife from pets (and pets from wildlife), the park requires all dogs to be on leashes no longer than 6 feet at all times. They are also not allowed on certain trails including the following: Fox Hollow, Stony Man, Limberlost, some Old Rag trails, Dark Hollow Falls, Story

A doe cares for her newborn fawn in the safety of Big Meadows.

of the Forest, Bearfence Mountain, and Frazier Discovery. Check with a park ranger for pet regulations or see the park website (www.nps.gov/shen/planyourvisit/pets.htm). Service dogs are permitted anywhere visitors can go.

Trails are marked with cement posts encircled with metal bands stamped with directions and mileage information, and also with colored paint blazes on trees or rocks that indicate the following: Appalachian Trail (white blaze), general hiking (blue blaze), a trail meant for both hiking and horseback riding (yellow blaze), and park boundary (red-orange blaze). A double blaze indicates a sharp turn or change in direction.

1. **Dickey Ridge/Fox Hollow Trail**—MP 4.6. Dickey Ridge is a great place to spot butterflies that nectar in the meadows of wildflowers. Look for spicebush swallowtails, great spangled fritillaries, and hackberry emperors. The Fox Hollow Trail is an interesting hike to an old homesite. Along the way you can spot spring wildflowers such as Jack-in-the-pulpit, cut-leaved toothwort, bloodroot, and showy orchis. When

you pass the piles of stones cleared by early settlers, make sure to look for the numerous chipmunks that use these rocky fortifications for shelter from predators. American goldfinches and American redstarts are common as are Carolina wrens and red-eyed vireos. Barred owls have also been spotted here, and white-tailed deer and black bears are frequently seen. In wet areas and along streams, you may see frogs jumping into the water and salamanders hiding under rocks and logs. Be cautious of northern copperheads that like to hide in similar areas.

2. **Hogback Overlook**—MP 20.8. Hogback Overlook is one of the overlooks in the park that allows a wide view to spy migrating hawks and eagles in the fall. Look for broadwings circling overhead in tornado-like kettles. They are often joined by vultures, red-tailed hawks, and bald eagles.

3. **Mathews Arm/Traces Trail**—MP 22.2. Black bears and white-tailed deer are frequently seen in the Mathews Arm area. The rocky areas near here are also favorite spots for timber rattlesnakes to hang out, so watch where you place your feet and hands. The Traces Trail is typical of deciduous woodlands where you can see oaks, hickories, and numerous mushrooms. An interesting wetland area at the head of the trail holds wetland plants such as cardinal flower, false hellebore, marsh violet, and marsh marigold. This is also a great place to look for birds, including hooded warblers, Acadian flycatchers, red-eyed vireos, gray catbirds, white-breasted nuthatches, ovenbirds, yellow-billed cuckoos, and wood thrushes. Butterflies include Appalachian tiger swallowtails in spring and later eastern tiger swallowtails, spicebush swallowtails, and fritillaries.

4. **Beahms Gap Area**—MP 28.5. In autumn this is one of the best places to spot fall migrants as well as resident forest birds. Listen for lots of eastern towhees calling to each other. The shrubby forest edges are great for spotting sparrows such as Lincoln's, swamp, song, and white-throated. Look for tiny golden-crowned kinglets and the spirited ruby-crowned kinglets flitting in the canopy. Woodpeckers that frequent the area include downy, red-bellied, and red-headed. In the parking area the mass of coralberry bushes provides shelter for cottontails and other small mammals. Look for insects such as grasshoppers and praying mantises hiding on the shrubbery. The orange berries near the forest edge are the nonnative oriental bittersweet. Bobcats have been spotted near here.

5. **Panorama**—MP 31.6. The Panorama area near the Thornton Gap Entrance station is the parking area for the popular Marys Rock Summit hike. Before your hike, take some time to enjoy the wildflowers in the open areas that attract lots of butterflies. Summer wildflowers include penstemon, black-eyed Susans, bounding bets, yellow jewelweeds,

Queen Anne's lace, yarrow, and flea-bane. Butterflies attracted to these nectar-filled flowers include tiger swallowtails, silver-spotted skippers, eastern-tailed blues, orange and clouded sulphurs, meadow fritillaries, and hummingbird moths. Eastern phoebes nest under the eaves of buildings, and you may see barn swallows zipping through the air catching insects on the fly. In the evenings, eastern cottontails munch on the tender grass in mowed areas along the Skyline Drive. Turkey vultures can often be seen here soaring overhead.

6. **Pinnacles Picnic Grounds**—MP 36.7. If you take your picnic lunch to the Pinnacles Picnic Grounds, you should also make sure to bring your binoculars. This is a great place to spot birds and other wildlife. In early morning, white-tailed deer graze on the lush grass while chipmunks scam-

You can visit Camp Hoover where President Hoover enjoyed fishing for the abundant trout in Shenandoah's pristine waters.

per about the grounds. Black bears are frequently seen here so make sure to keep your food items attended or locked in your car. Some of the birds found here include white-breasted nuthatches, American goldfinches, brown thrashers, eastern wood-pewees, eastern bluebirds, blue-headed vireos, and indigo buntings.

7. **Stony Man Overlook**—MP 38.5. This overlook offers a great view of Stony Man, the second highest peak in the park. It was named for its resemblance to the profile of a man's face when viewed from a distance. At the Stony Man Overlook, the panoramic view into the Shenandoah Valley is also great for spying birds, including peregrine falcons, common ravens, hawks, and vultures. Wildflowers here include common milkweed, wild bergamot, yarrow, crown vetch, and sweet white clover, many of which attract butterflies, including monarchs, fritillaries, and skippers.

8. **Stony Man Trail**—MP 41.7. This popular trail has a trail guide, available at the trailhead, that corresponds to numbered posts along the trail. You can see mountain laurel, northern red oak, yellow birch, mountain ash, red spruce, and balsam fir along the trail. Boreal life zone species such as three-toothed cinquefoil and Michaux's saxifrage also grow here. At 4,010 feet in elevation, the greenstone cliffs of Stony Man summit comprise the second-highest elevation in Shenandoah with great views into the Shenandoah Valley below and the Massanutten and Allegheny Mountains beyond. The high-elevation plant communities here

The federally endangered Shenandoah salamander is found nowhere else in the world except in Shenandoah National Park.

are considered globally rare and threatened by human trampling impacts. Please stay on the trail to avoid stepping on these and other plants. Watch for soaring hawks, such as broad-winged and red-tailed hawks. Other birds to look for include blue-headed vireos, scarlet tanagers, dark-eyed juncos, and eastern towhees.

9. **Millers Head Trail**—MP 42.5. Millers Head Trail begins near the Skyland amphitheater and winds its way 0.8 mile to an observation platform with a spectacular viewpoint of the Shenandoah Valley. This is also a great place to spot raptors flying past, such as red-tailed and red-shouldered hawks. Although rated as an easy hike, hiking/trekking poles can help you navigate your steps; this trail is rocky and a bit steep in places, but the pleasing viewpoint at the end and the bountiful spring wildflowers in early May are a pleasant reward. Along the trail you can find wildflowers including golden ragwort, purple clematis, large-flowered trillium, and early saxifrage. Look for birds, such as red-eyed vireos, Carolina chickadees, and eastern towhees.

10. **Limberlost**—MP 43. What was once a unique forest of giant hemlocks has been devastatingly transformed by the work of a tiny nonnative insect called the hemlock woolly adelgid. The Limberlost Trail is seeing rapid succession and growth of beautiful groves

of mountain laurel. Woodland flowers such as pink lady's-slippers, false hellebore, and violets can be seen. This is also a great place to look for mushrooms along the trail. Gray squirrels, chipmunks, and black bears are frequently seen here. Open areas along the trail make it easier to see birds, including scarlet tanagers, hooded warblers, chestnut-sided warblers, ovenbirds, great crested flycatchers, and red-eyed vireos.

11. **Franklin Cliffs**—MP 49. Franklin Cliffs is a short but sweet trail to a cliff overlooking the Shenandoah Valley. In early spring, wildflowers such as wild pink, moss phlox, and heart-leaved Alexander can be found along the 5-minute trail to the cliff. Look for birds, including American redstarts, chestnut-sided warblers, eastern towhees, rose-breasted grosbeaks, scarlet tanagers, ovenbirds, and pileated woodpeckers.

12. **Hawksbill Summit**—MP 45.6. Soaring to an elevation of 4,051 feet, Hawksbill is the highest point in the park. This high peak supports plants more typically found north of Virginia, including a wide assortment of ferns, mosses, lichens, and wildflowers such as yellow bead lily. Stay on the trail and watch where you place your feet to avoid trampling these and other sensitive high-elevation plants. Birds, such as vultures, ravens, and peregrine falcons, soar on the winds.

13. **Big Meadows**—MP 51. The Big Meadows area is one of the best places in the park to see an abundance of wildlife. White-tailed deer are especially plentiful here and graze peacefully in the meadow in the early morning and late evening. Red-shouldered hawks, northern harriers, and common ravens soar over the meadow hunting for prey. Eastern bluebirds hunt from weedy perches for their insect prey. Sparrows include chipping, field, and song sparrows. Insects feast on the abundant wildflowers and heath shrubs, such as maleberry, black huckleberry, and blueberries that cover the meadow. If you look carefully along the paths, you may be able to spot the rare leathery grape fern in late summer and fall. Big Meadows is the only place in Virginia where gray birch can be seen. In this high-elevation meadow you can also see other unusual Virginia plants, including the white, wand-like flowers of devils bit and fly poison. Colorful flowers such as asters, common milkweed, and butterfly milkweed attract myriad butterflies. Look for eastern tiger swallowtails, American coppers, great spangled fritillaries, and a host of other butterflies here. Black bears, coyotes, raccoons, and skunks may be seen in the evening and at night. The nearby Dark Hollow Falls trailhead at milepost 50.7 is also a good place to spot black bears.

14. **Milam Gap/Mill Prong Trail/Rapidan Camp**—MP 52.8. At Milam Gap you can see remnants of old apple orchards that once covered this area. Look for British soldier lichens on the old wooden fence at the parking area. Broad-winged hawks nest in the

Big Meadows supports the globally rare Northern Blue Ridge mafic fen plant community.

area and feed on snakes, including red-bellied snakes. The Mill Prong Trail is great for beautiful spring wildflowers, including violets, showy orchis, rosy-twisted stalk, and miterwort. The trail leads past a wetland where you can see false hellebore, wild lettuce, and turtlehead. Follow the trail farther to Rapidan Camp, where you might spot brook trout swimming in the cool mountain streams. Northern water snakes bask in the open areas here and along the Rapidan River. Along the way, look for warblers, such as hooded, Blackburnian, Canada, and northern parulas. American redstarts, ruby-crowned kinglets, scarlet tanagers, and blue-headed vireos may also be seen. Listen for the flute-like song of the wood thrush and the "teacher-teacher" call of the ovenbird.

15. **South River Falls**—MP 62.8. With a drop of 83 feet in two stages, this is the third-highest falls in the park. A popular hike with numerous switchbacks, you can see wildflowers, including violets, blue cohosh, wild geraniums, Jack-in-the-pulpit, and many other species that occur in rich woods. Look for gray squirrels and chipmunks along the trail. Stay on the trail to avoid trampling the vegetation and prevent unnecessary erosion. Birding is good here, so keep an eye out for Carolina chickadees, kinglets, indigo buntings, and vireos as well as colorful rose-breasted grosbeaks, scarlet tanagers, and many warblers, including black-throated blues, black-and-whites, and ceruleans.

16. **Loft Mountain area**—MP 79.5. White-tailed deer are abundant here, and black bears are also frequently sighted in the wooded areas. Gray catbirds, northern cardinals, and American goldfinches can be seen in the campground. Along the Frazier Discovery Trail, you can see eastern towhees and black-and-white, hooded, and worm-eating warblers.

17. **Blackrock Summit**—MP 84.8. Here you can see the fascinating geological features of rocky talus quartzite. This is a great place to see lichens, such as the black toadskin rock tripe that gives this summit its name. Lichens take a long time to grow and can be quickly damaged or destroyed by footsteps. Watch for camouflaged wolf and other hunting spiders that are the same color as the rocks and lichens. Eastern fence lizards and five-lined skinks can be seen dashing about the rocks. Be mindful that timber rattlesnakes like rocky areas such as this for shelter and sunning. Soaring hawks, ravens, and vultures are easily seen from the sky-top view here. Look for other bird species, including hooded warblers, American redstarts, blue-headed vireos, and pileated woodpeckers.

18. **Beagle Gap**—MP 99.5. The open wildflower-filled meadows on both sides of Skyline Drive are great for spotting butterflies and other insects. Watch for crab spiders and ambush bugs that nestle in the flowers waiting to grab an unsuspecting bee or other insect. Apple trees attract deer, and black bears and wild turkeys frequent the area. This is also a great place to watch for soaring black and turkey vultures and raptors, such as broad-winged, Cooper's, sharp-shinned, and red-tailed hawks. At nearby Jarman Gap (milepost 96.8), you can see a great selection of woodland ferns including Christmas fern, ebony spleenwort, maidenhair fern, polypody, and woodland species of grape ferns.

Ecosystems

Shenandoah covers 198,400 acres of the Blue Ridge Mountains and protects many rare and threatened habitats in Virginia. The mixed deciduous forests of this northern Blue Ridge ecosystem are globally significant and include over 79,579 acres of designated wilderness. About 96 percent of the park is forested, and about 4 percent is made up of special communities, including wetlands and barrens. The Blue Ridge Mountains are part of the long chain of ancient Appalachian Mountains that stretch from Alabama into Newfoundland. The Appalachians contain some of the most biologically diverse habitats in the United States. With an elevation range from 595 feet at Front Royal to 4,050 feet at Hawksbill Summit, the diversity of flora and fauna is wide ranging. More than 1,400 species of vascular plants have been identified here. The cool mountain streams provide habitat for native brook

Once as tall as the Rocky Mountains, the Appalachians have eroded over billions of years into gentle rolling mountains.

trout, and the talus slopes of three tall peaks shelter the world's only population of the Shenandoah salamander. The globally significant natural resources provide habitat for nesting birds, including neotropical migrants and the world's fastest bird, the peregrine falcon. Forests are recovering from farming and timber harvesting, and white-tailed deer and black bears have made a very successful comeback from overhunting.

About 11,000 years ago, glaciers covered land as close as Pennsylvania to the north but did not reach Virginia. Some of the northern species that were forced south by the glaciers remain in the Blue Ridge on the high, cool mountain peaks, including balsam fir, red spruce, Canada yew, red-breasted nuthatch, and winter wren. In the central section of the park, Big Meadows is a 121-acre high-elevation meadow that supports a globally rare plant association or community called the Northern Blue Ridge mafic fen. The greenstone rock cliffs on the tallest mountains support another globally rare plant community called the high-elevation greenstone outcrop barren association. The rock outcrops also provide habitat for diverse plants and animals. The significant lichen populations in the park are unique, and a species new to science has been discovered here.

Doe with fawn

Buck

WHITE-TAILED DEER
Odocoileus virginianus
Deer family (Cervidae)

Quick ID: reddish-tan in summer, grayish-brown in winter; white around eyes and nose; white throat, stomach, and underside of tail; males have antlers, females are without antlers

Length: 3–7.8' Weight: 120–297 lbs

Early colonists to the area depended on deer as an important source of food and clothing, and deer were eventually hunted to near extinction in Virginia. In 1934, thirteen deer were brought in from the Mount Vernon Estate and successfully released along the Big Run in the southern section of the soon-to-be Shenandoah National Park. By 1955, the offspring of these and other deer from several nearby restocking efforts resulted in numbers that reached roughly 600 deer. In recent years the numbers have soared into the thousands. Big Meadows is a great place to view deer, especially in the early morning and at twilight as they come into the meadow to graze. Remember that even though deer may seem tame, they are wild animals and can kick and bite. Touching, feeding, or hunting any animal in the park is illegal.

COYOTE
Canis latrans
Dog family (Canidae)
Quick ID: medium size, doglike, gray to reddish coat, pointed erect ears, long slender snout, black-tipped tail usually carried straight down

Length: 2.5–3.3' Weight: 15–50 lbs

Coyotes have expanded their range from the western states to the eastern states. A recent addition to the mammal list for the park, coyotes can now be seen with regularity. Very adaptable, the coyote can flourish in a wide variety of habitats, including eastern forests with abundant food sources. Coyotes feed mainly on small mammals, including rodents and rabbits, but will also eat a wide variety of plants, fruits, and carrion. Opportunistic and intelligent, they soon discovered that human food and garbage may be easily obtained and will take advantage of unsecured picnic leftovers. Coyotes have been seen in the Big Meadows area and near Skyland. Please never feed any wild animal in the park and make sure to store food and garbage in wildlife-proof containers.

GRAY FOX
Urocyon cinereoargenteus
Dog family (Canidae)
Quick ID: salt-and-pepper grizzled gray back with dark streak on back and tail; black-tipped tail; rusty side, neck, legs, and feet

Length: 21–29" Weight: 7–13 lbs

These small nocturnal foxes are often mistaken for red foxes, but they are smaller and have a black-tipped tail rather than the white-tipped tail of the red fox. Gray foxes have a unique ability to climb trees, which sets them apart from other members of the canine family. They use their claws to climb into trees to forage for fruits and to escape danger. Most active at dusk and dawn, they are sometime seen foraging for insects and small mammals.

RED FOX
Vulpes vulpes
Dog family (Canidae)
Quick ID: small, doglike, reddish coat, white underneath, white-tipped bushy tail

Length: 2.7–3.6' Weight: 7–15 lbs

The red fox is found throughout most of Virginia and its preferred habitats include open forests, brushy fields, and farmlands. In Shenandoah National Park, the red fox is mostly found at lower elevations. Although weighing only about ten pounds, the full coat of the red fox makes it look bigger than it really is. Using their keen eyesight, hearing, and sense of smell, foxes usually hunt in the late evening and early morning hours and will eat a wide variety of food, including small mammals, birds, insects, berries, and plant material. Well known for their intelligence, foxes sometimes use defense tactics such as backtracking or turning in circles to confuse predators.

BOBCAT
Lynx rufus
Cat family (Felidae)
Quick ID: tawny to gray with black spots and bars, black ear tufts, short tail

Length: 1.5–3.54' Weight: 8.4–45 lbs

A fairly common resident of the park, bobcats are rarely seen, as they are secretive hunters of the night. The cats are active at dawn and dusk, and their keen senses of sight and smell help them locate prey, such as rodents and other small mammals. Alert drivers at night can sometimes catch a glimpse of these well-camouflaged animals dashing across Skyline Drive or hopping onto the stone guard wall before dashing to the safety of the dark woodlands. They are active all year and seek shelter in hollow trees and brush or rock piles.

STRIPED SKUNK
Mephitis mephitis
Skunk family (Mephitidae)
Quick ID: black with 2 broad white stripes along back, large bushy tail with variable black and white

Length: 22–31.5" Weight: 6–10 lbs

Commonly called "polecats," skunks are one of the most well-recognized creatures of the animal world and are renowned for their foul-smelling defense mechanism. Skunks forage at night for insects and plant materials and will readily get into unsecured food or garbage. Skunks are preyed upon by hawks and owls. Unlucky victims of a blast of skunk spray can find relief by washing with a mixture of 3 percent hydrogen peroxide, a quarter cup of baking soda, and some liquid dishwashing soap, but the concoction may change hair color. The home remedy of bathing in tomato juice only masks the scent. The uncommon smaller spotted skunk stands on its front feet before spraying.

EASTERN SPOTTED SKUNK
Spilogale putorius
Skunk family (Mephitidae)
Quick ID: broken white stripes on black back, white spot on forehead, white spot in front of each ear, bushy black tail with white tip

Length: 14–21.4" Weight: 0.5–4 lbs

These unusual skunks have a ferret-like shape and elongated white blotches that resemble large spots. Unlike the striped skunk, which lifts its tail before spraying, the spotted skunk performs an acrobatic handstand before spraying its victim with a noxious, foul-smelling, oily secretion that can be projected over 4 yards away. They also warn potential predators by stamping their feet on the ground. Spotted skunks were traditionally called civet cats and are omnivorous, dining on small rodents, lizards, grubs, and insects as well as berries and other vegetation. The larger striped skunk often has such variable white stripes that it can easily be mistaken for a spotted skunk.

RACCOON
Procyon lotor
Raccoon family (Procyonidae)
Quick ID: grizzled brownish gray, stocky body, pointed snout, black facial mask, 5 to 7 black rings on bushy 8- to 12-inch-long tail

Length: 18–28" Weight: 4–23 lbs

The distinguishing black mask across the eyes and a bushy tail with black rings are characteristic marks of a raccoon. Highly adaptable and noted for their intelligence, raccoons have expanded their range from eastern woodlands to urban areas and farmlands across North America and into northern South America. Raccoons are often seen near lodges and campgrounds in Shenandoah. Primarily nocturnal, raccoons are omnivores and eat a variety of fruits and plant materials as well as small mammals and invertebrates such as insects or crayfish. Watch for raccoons near culverts under roads, where they can find shelter and dine on the many small creatures, such as rodents and salamanders, traveling through the culverts.

Black bear with
mange

BLACK BEAR
Ursus americanus
Bear family (Ursidae)
Quick ID: large, usually black to brownish, light brown snout, round ears, flat-footed walk

Length: 4–6.5' Weight: 86–700 lbs

The excitement of seeing a large predator in the wild, especially a black bear, is a highlight for many visitors to Shenandoah National Park. By the early 1900s black bears had been essentially eliminated from the area around the park, but through conservation efforts of biologists, and the protection provided by the national park, black bears now enjoy a thriving population in the park and surrounding counties. Black bears are primarily vegetarians and eat a wide variety of plants, berries, and nuts, but can quickly learn that human food and garbage make an easy meal. Picnickers and campers in the park are required to safely store their food, use bear-proof garbage containers, and never attempt to feed bears. Some black bears in the park have contracted a contagious skin disease called mange. It is caused by mites and causes relentless itching resulting in fur loss, and dry skin. Park regulations require that you stay at least 50 yards from bears. Bears are found throughout the park and may be seen crossing Skyline Drive. Always make noise while hiking to avoid surprising a bear, but if you do spot one, keep your children close to you and back away slowly (see Safety Notes pp. 8–10).

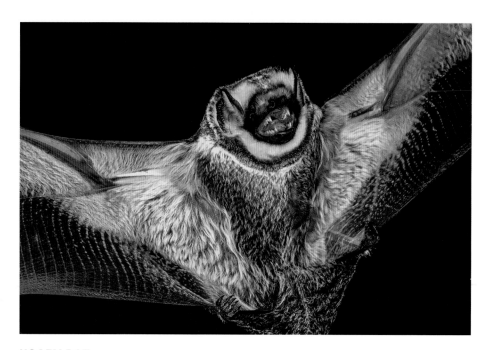

HOARY BAT
Lasiurus cinereus
Evening Bats and Vesper Bats family (Vespertilionidae)
Quick ID: brown fur with silvery frosted tips, yellow throat, outer portion of wings darker than inner portion

Length: 5.12–5.91" Weight: 0.7–1.23 oz

With a wingspan of almost 17 inches, the hoary bat is the largest bat in the region. Another large bat, the big brown bat (*Eptesicus fuscus*), has a wingspan of about 13 inches and can be seen flying over meadows and campgrounds along with little brown bats (*Myotis lucifugus*), eastern pipistrelles (*Pipistrellus subflavus*), and red bats (*Lasiurus borealis*). The seventeen species of bats found in Virginia play an important role in the ecosystem because they eat a large number of insects nightly. Owls prey on bats at night, and hawks will take bats in flight during migration. Bats are now threatened by a fungal disease called "white-nose syndrome," which has greatly reduced populations of certain bat species, especially those that hibernate in caves.

BIG BROWN BAT
Eptesicus fuscus
Evening Bats and Vesper Bats family (Vespertilionidae)
Quick ID: brownish fur, broad nose, fleshy lips, rounded ears, wingspan about 13 inches; females are slightly larger than males

Length: 4.5-5" Weight: 0.81 oz

Resting during the day, these night workers zero in on their flying insect prey and play a major role in keeping the insect population in check. Bats use ultrasonic vocal signals as echolocation to find their prey. This echolocation enables bats to detect prey and avoid obstacles. To help determine the species of bat, researchers use the unique shape of the tragus, which is the fleshy piece of skin in front of the ear canal. Depending on the species, the tragus can be rounded (as in the big brown bat) or triangular or pointed. The favorite food of the big brown bat is beetles, and it uses its strong jaws to chew the hard exoskeleton. Baby bats, called pups, are raised in maternity colonies and the babies stay together while their mothers forage at night. Big brown bats can live up to 19 years in the wild. These and other bats can sometimes be seen sleeping undisturbed under the eaves of buildings or other structures. About 20 minutes after sunset, you can watch the aerial maneuvers of bats over Big Meadows and around light posts as they zip expertly through to catch the moths and other insects that are attracted to the light.

VIRGINIA OPOSSUM
Didelphis virginiana
Opossum family (Didelphidae)
Quick ID: grizzled gray; white face; pointed snout; black, pink-tipped ears; long hairless tail

Length: 15–20" Weight: 9–13 lbs

With many smaller cousins in South America, the Virginia opossum is the only marsupial found in North America north of Mexico. Females have a fur-lined pouch where they carry their typically seven to nine young that affix to the nipples for about two months. Well known for their defense tactic of pretending to be dead, Virginia opossums go into a catatonic state when threatened, becoming limp and falling to the ground. This is commonly called "playing possum" and is used colloquially for feigning sleep. According to a 1929 story, when presented with a live opossum from a local boy, in return President Herbert Hoover arranged for a new school to be built in the area near Camp Rapidan.

EASTERN COTTONTAIL
Sylvilagus floridanus
Rabbit family (Leporidae)
Quick ID: rusty gray-brown fur, underside fur white, large hind feet, long ears, short fluffy white tail, rusty patch on nape of neck

Length: 14–17" Weight: 2–4 lbs

Eastern cottontails play an important role in the food chain, as many predators rely on these small mammals for sustenance. Cottontails, commonly called rabbits, comprise from 50 to 75 percent of the diet of foxes and bobcats in certain habitats. Rabbits have a high reproductive rate, and a buck (male) and doe (female) can produce twenty-five rabbits per year; without predators these prolific breeders would soon overrun their habitat resources. Early settlers and American Indians also relied on rabbits to feed themselves and their families, and many pioneer recipes for stews included wild game such as rabbits, squirrels, groundhogs, or opossums as the main ingredient. They also relied on rabbit fur sewn together for warm clothing and blankets.

Meadow vole

SOUTHERN RED-BACKED VOLE
Myodes gapperi
Mice, Rat, and Vole family (Cricetidae)
Quick ID: dark gray with chestnut-brown strip on back, face and sides yellowish brown, underparts whitish, short tail

Length: 2.76–4.41" Weight: 0.21–1.48 oz

It is often the quiet, unseen forest inhabitants that play a major role in the ecological food web. Although tiny in size, voles are one of the most important members of the food chain, as many predators, such as hawks, owls, and foxes, rely on them for sustenance. Their reproductive rate is high; females have two to three litters of one to eleven young each year, and voles are capable of mating at three months of age. They eat a variety of food, including plants, fungi, nuts, seeds, and occasionally insects. Their average life span in the wild is about one year. Southern red-backed voles are typically found at high elevations in the park. The meadow vole (*Microtus pennsylvanicus*) is the most common vole in the park, and if you are lucky, you may spot one scampering across trails in Big Meadows.

ALLEGHENY WOODRAT
Neotoma magister
Mice, Rat, and Vole family (Cricetidae)
Quick ID: brownish-gray, black-tipped hairs on upper body; underside and feet white; 6-inch hairy tail white underneath

Length: 8–9" Weight: 7–13.5 oz

Woodrats are similar in size to house rats but have hairy rather than scaly tails and soft, fine fur. With large dark eyes, rounded ears, and blunt snouts, they look a bit like a big hamster with a long tail. Also known as "packrats" or "trade rats," these hoarders will collect shiny and colorful objects such as bottle caps, coins, or rings and in their place leave a stick, pine cone, or nut. The range of the Allegheny woodrat extends from Pennsylvania to Tennessee along the Appalachian Mountains. In several states, including Virginia, they are listed as a species of concern due to a population decline.

WHITE-FOOTED MOUSE
Peromyscus leucopus
Mice, Rat, and Vole family (Cricetidae)
Quick ID: grayish to reddish-brown, yellowish wash on sides, white underparts, white feet, long bicolored tail, large beady eyes, large round ears

Length: body 3.6–4.2", tail: 2–5"
Weight: 0.66–1.25 oz

The white-footed mouse and the closely related deer mouse (*P. maniculatus*) are common inhabitants of the park. White-footed mice can live in a wide variety of habitats but are often found at the edges of meadows and in forests. Active year-round, they are an important food source for many other animals, including owls, hawks, snakes, foxes, and other predators. Females have a high reproductive rate and may have many litters of four to six young per year. They eat insects as well as seeds and nuts that they store in caches for winter use.

Deer mouse

WOODLAND JUMPING MOUSE
Napaeozapus insignis
Jumping Mice family (Dipodidae)
Quick ID: dark brown back, yellowish sides, whitish belly, large hind feet, 5- to 6-inch-long tail with white tip

Length: 3.75–4" Weight: 0.6–1.23 oz

Like a miniature kangaroo, the woodland jumping mouse has extremely strong legs that allow it to jump nearly 10 feet when alarmed. Its tail, which is longer than its body, acts as a rudder to help it maintain balance in midair. Mainly nocturnal, jumping mice rest under vegetation during the day, then forage by night on insects, seeds, fungi, and fruits. In an important symbiotic relationship, the woodland jumping mouse feeds on an underground fungus called *Endogone,* helping to spread the spores of the fungus. The meadow jumping mouse (*Zapus hudsonius*), which is usually found in open areas, is larger, looks more reddish on the sides, and does not have the white tip on the tail.

SOUTHERN FLYING SQUIRREL
Glaucomys volans
Squirrel family (Sciuridae)
Quick ID: greyish-brown fur on top, light cream underneath, large dark eyes, flattened tail, furry membrane between front and rear legs

Length: 8.35–0.12" Weight: 1.62–3 oz

Even though southern flying squirrels have the word "flying" in their name, bats are the only mammals that can truly fly. Flying squirrels have a flap of loose skin that extends from their front to their rear legs. When they leap from tree to tree, they spread their arms and legs and the furred membrane is extended into a living sail and their flattened tail acts as an effective rudder. When they land, they immediately move to the other side of the tree to avoid predators, such as owls, that may have spotted their nocturnal glide. From a height of about 60 feet up, they can glide about 165 feet before coming in for a landing. The favorite food of flying squirrels are the underground mushrooms called truffles, and the squirrels help spread the fungal spores.

WOODCHUCK
Marmota monax
Squirrel family (Sciuridae)
Quick ID: brownish-gray heavy body, short legs, tail about 5 inches long

Length: 16–20" Weight: 5–10 lbs

Woodchucks are commonly seen nibbling on the tender grass that grows along Skyline Drive. They often sit upright, watching out for danger, and scamper to safety as cars pass by. Locally they are called "groundhogs" as not only do they eat over one-third of their body weight per day, but they also dig large underground burrows that are 4 to 5 feet deep and 14 to 30 feet long. Groundhogs hibernate from October to February, but may rouse on warm days to browse for food. Another name for woodchucks is "whistlepig," because they sound a shrill whistle when alarmed. Groundhogs were routinely hunted by early residents, providing a welcome meal of roast or stew.

Red Squirrel

GRAY SQUIRREL
Sciurus carolinensis
Squirrel family (Sciuridae)

Quick ID: salt-and-pepper gray back and bushy tail, brown sides, white underparts

Length: body 8–10", tail 8–10" Weight: 9–17 oz

In Virginia, gray squirrels are common woodland inhabitants and may be seen in a wide variety of habitats in Shenandoah. The closely related fox squirrels (*S. niger*) are larger and have luxuriant silvery-reddish fur, but we have only seen them near the North Entrance in the park. The smaller red squirrels (*Tamiasciurus hudsonicus*) have reddish-brown fur and are typically found in high-elevation conifers such as those on Hawksbill summit. Gray squirrels gather nuts and hide them in many scattered places for the long winters. Each squirrel may bury a thousand nuts each season. They have excellent memories and can recognize the location of these caches as well as find them using their sense of smell. Gray squirrels build a twig and leaf nest, called a drey, in the forks of trees.

EASTERN CHIPMUNK
Tamias striatus
Squirrel family (Sciuridae)
Quick ID: small reddish-brown, one white stripe on each side bordered by black, creamy white broken eye ring

Length: 5–6" Weight: 2½–4½ oz

Resembling miniature striped squirrels, eastern chipmunks entertain visitors to the park with their constant motion as they search for food. Chipmunks tend to forage close to protective shelter, including shrubs, rock piles, rock walls, buildings, and cabins. Unlike many animals that are active at dawn or dusk, chipmunks are most active in the afternoon when their stripes on their back blend well with afternoon shadows, thus providing them with better protection from predators such as hawks and ravens that patrol the ground for potential prey. During the fall they busily store nuts and seeds in underground burrows where they spend the winter in a state of torpor, waking about twice a week to grab a mid-winter snack. Fox Hollow Trail is a great place to spot chipmunks as they dart around the crumbling stone fences.

RED-SHOULDERED HAWK
Buteo lineatus
Hawks, Eagles, and Kites family (Accipitridae)
Quick ID: dark wings with white checkered pattern, rusty-red shoulders, translucent buffy crescent across wingtips, rusty-red barring across white underparts

Length: 17" Weight: 1.4 lbs Wingspan: 40"

Red-shouldered hawks often perch in tall trees at the edges of meadows or open spaces, intently surveying the ground for small mammals, amphibians, or reptiles. They can sometimes be seen soaring over Big Meadows and can be quite vocal. Red-shoulders are permanent residents but will descend to the warmer valleys in colder months. Cooper's hawks (*Accipiter cooperii*) have much longer tails and shorter wings than red-shouldered hawks. Red-tailed hawks are larger with a red tail and dark bellyband. Northern harriers (*Circus hudsonius*) have a white rump.

Nest with young

RED-TAILED HAWK
Buteo jamaicensis
Hawks, Eagles, and Kites family (Accipitridae)
Quick ID: large, brown, broad rounded wings; broad reddish tail; streaked bellyband

Length: 19" Weight: 2.4 lbs Wingspan: 49"

One of the most common hawks in North America, red-tailed hawks are often the first hawk identified by novice birders. Red-tailed hawks have a characteristic rusty-red tail and a darkly streaked bellyband. In contrast, red-shouldered hawks have red barring covering their belly and a distinctly barred tail. Female northern harriers (*Circus hudsonius*) have vertical brown belly streaks, while males are pale gray on the back. Red-tails and other raptors can be seen flying past overlooks in the park and cruising over landmarks such as Old Rag, Stony Man, and Hawksbill. Open fields such as Big Meadows are also good places to spot these and other hawks hunting for small mammals.

Kettle of broad-wings

BROAD-WINGED HAWK
Buteo platypterus
Hawks, Eagles, and Kites family (Accipitridae)
Quick ID: small with rusty striped breast, light underwings, 3 to 4 thick black-and-white stripes on short tail

Length: 15" Weight: 14 oz Wingspan: 34"

One of the most spectacular occurrences in nature is the migration of the broad-winged hawk. Drawn together by the ancient call of the species, in mid to late September thousands of broad-wings begin the long migration to their tropical wintering grounds. Rising high on warm air currents, the hawks soar over the mountains in huge tornado-like spirals known as "kettles." Birders can see these and other migrants especially well at gaps in the mountains; the southern terminus of the park at Rockfish Gap near Waynesboro is one such regular migratory passageway. Broad-wings and other migrating raptors can also be seen at overlooks in the park, including those at Hogback and Stony Man and at Hawksbill Mountain and the Beagle Gap area. A great way to learn about hawk identification is to visit a hawk watch in fall. At the southern end of Shenandoah, the Rockfish Gap hawk watch is in Waynesboro, Virginia. Bring your binoculars and you can listen to experts call out their names as you watch raptors soaring just overhead in their annual migration. You can find details about this and other hawk migration counts online at the Hawk Migration Association of North America at hawkcount.org.

Sharp-shinned hawk

Sharp-shinned hawk in flight

COOPER'S HAWK
Accipiter cooperii
Hawks, Eagles, and Kites family (Accipitridae)
Quick ID: medium-sized hawk, steely-gray above, warm reddish horizontal bars on underparts, broad rounded wings, long rounded tail with thick banding and white tip, head appears large

Length: 16.5" Weight: 1 lb Wingspan: 31"

Silent stealthy predators, Cooper's hawks expertly maneuver through forests at breakneck speed when in pursuit of their prey—other birds. A skilled woodland hunter, they can sometimes be seen flying over Big Meadows with a characteristic flap-flap-guide flight. Often presenting an identification challenge for many birders, the smaller sharp-shinned hawk (*A. striatus*) is very similar in appearance to the Cooper's hawk. Females of both species are typically much larger than males. By observing field marks such as shape and size, with experience, you can usually tell these two accipiters apart. Cooper's hawks are crow sized while "sharpies" are smaller than a crow but larger than a robin or blue jay. Complicating the identification, large female sharpies often approach the size of small male Cooper's hawk. Cooper's hawks have a rounded tail and large head, which extends beyond the wings in flight. Sharp-shinned hawks have a small "tucked in" head in flight and a straight edged tail.

NORTHERN HARRIER
Circus hudsonius
Hawks, Eagles, and Kites family (Accipitridae)
Quick ID: long broad wings, long tail with blackish bands, white rump, flat owl-like face with facial disk of short stiff feathers around each eye, hooked bill; males are gray above, whitish below; females are larger than males, and are brown with whitish underside with brown streaks

Length: 18" Weight: 15 oz Wingspan: 43"

Seasoned birdwatchers may refer to a northern harrier as a "marsh hawk," as that was the common name many of us learned for this bird in years past. In a group known as "harriers," these raptors are the only member of this genus found in North America. Graceful fliers, northern harriers soar slowly over open meadows, fields, and marshes intently hunting for small mammals, reptiles, amphibians, and small birds. Slowly gliding in hunting mode, they tend to hold their wings in a V-shape, or dihedral, often teetering from side to side. As well as the flight tendencies, look for the distinctive white rump on both male and female. Smaller than females, males are silvery gray, while females and young males are brown. Great listeners, their owl-like facial disk of short feathers helps direct any sounds from potential prey to their keen ears. Effective at keeping rodent populations in check, these hawks are welcomed by farmers in the valleys surrounding the park. Look for northern harriers in Big Meadows or along ridges in migration.

TURKEY VULTURE
Cathartes aura
New World Vulture family (Cathartidae)

Black vulture

Quick ID: black with silvery flight feathers, bare red head, flies with wings in dihedral

Length: 25.2–31.9" Weight: 4 lbs Wingspan: 67–70"

Soaring on the breeze, turkey vultures are often seen from overlooks along Skyline Drive. They are frequently mistaken for hawks or eagles and even have the nickname "mountain eagle." Another common nickname is "turkey buzzard" or simply "buzzard," but they are not related to the hawks called buzzards that are found in Europe and Africa. Turkey vultures soar with their wings held in a shallow "V shape"—called a dihedral—as they search for food using an extremely heightened sense of smell to locate carrion. They have pale silvery areas along the back portion of their outstretched wings. Black vultures (*Coragyps atratus*) have pale areas at the ends of their wings and fly with their wings straight with rigorous flapping. You can see both species of vultures soaring over most overlooks along Skyline Drive, including Bacon Hollow Overlook, Hogback Overlook, and Stonyman Overlook.

American kestrel

PEREGRINE FALCON
Falco peregrinus
Falcon family (Falconidae)
Quick ID: large and stocky, gray barring, black cap, black moustache, long pointed wings; males and females alike in coloration; females larger than males

Length: 16" Weight: 1.6 lbs Wingspan: 41"

Peregrine falcons historically nested on the craggy rock faces in Shenandoah, but in the 1960s their numbers plummeted due to the widespread use of pesticides, especially DDT. Thanks to public outcry and the conservation efforts of biologists and bird banders who record numbers and species of birds, peregrines recovered in most of their range and in 1999 were removed from the Federal Endangered Species List. Peregrine numbers are stable in coastal and urban areas of the mid-Atlantic region. In the Central Appalachians, however, they have seen a much slower recovery. Hopefully they will soon return to their dominant role as top predator in the skies over Shenandoah. Peregrines are the fastest flying bird in the world, and in a straight dive can reach speeds up to 200 miles per hour. Look for peregrines in the Skyland area and at overlooks such as Crescent Rock and Stonyman. About half the size of the peregrine, American kestrels (*F. sparverius*) have a reddish back and tail.

Eastern screech owl

Great horned owl

BARRED OWL
Strix varia
Owl family (Strigidae)
Quick ID: large, gray-brown back with white mottled markings, lacks ear tufts, pale gray facial disc, black eyes, horizontal bars on head and neck, vertical brown-streaked white belly

Length: 21" Weight: 1.6 lbs Wingspan: 42"

The barred owl is a large owl with a rounded head and dark eyes. It lacks the ear tufts of the larger great horned owl (*Bubo virginianus*). It has one of the most recognizable of all bird calls as it seems to say, "who cooks for you, who cooks for you all," with the last syllable descending and drawn out. The barred owl may be active during the day, and you may find one perched on a tree limb listening for the scamper of prey in the underbrush. Besides the great horned owl, the other owl that breeds in the park is the much smaller eastern screech owl (*Megascops asio*). Barred owls are frequently seen along Fox Hollow Trail, Blackrock Summit Trail, Limberlost, and Little Devil Stairs Overlook.

47

RUFFED GROUSE
Bonasa umbellus
Upland Game Bird family (Phasianidae)
Quick ID: chicken-like, gray or rufous with dark mottling and bars, rounded wings and tail, black band on tail, short crest on head, feather ruffs on sides of neck

Length: 17" Weight: 1.3 lbs Wingspan: 22"

So camouflaged are the mottled feathers of the ruffed grouse that spotting one in the woods is quite difficult. Typically, either you will hear them first or they will surprise you by blasting off in a loud flurry when you get too close. They tend to stay in quiet forests where there is plenty of cover but may sometimes be seen crossing Skyline Drive or quietly foraging for insects by a woodland trail. In spring males advertise their presence to females in a process called "drumming." They strut along a suitable fallen log, proudly spreading their tail and displaying their feathers, then begin swimming their wings rapidly through the air, producing a drumming sound that attracts females for mating.

WILD TURKEY
Meleagris gallopavo
Upland Game Bird family (Phasianidae)
Quick ID: dark brown body, unfeathered bluish head with red markings and wattles, brown tail with buffy tips

Length: 37–46" Weight: 9–16 lbs Wingspan: 50–64"

If Benjamin Franklin had his way, the wild turkey would be our national symbol rather than the bald eagle. An important source of food for American Indians and early settlers, wild turkeys were eliminated from much of the east by the early 1900s. Reintroduction programs were implemented, and today turkeys enjoy the protection of Shenandoah. During the day they can be found grazing in the meadows and woodlands, and at night they roost in the safety of trees. In spring you can watch female hens followed by a line of up to seventeen awkward young pecking at the ground for insects and seeds. Two other ground-dwelling, camouflaged but smaller birds in the park are the ruffed grouse (*Bonasa umbellus*) and the American woodcock (*Scolopax minor*).

AMERICAN WOODCOCK
Scolopax minor
Sandpipers and Allies family (Scolopacidae)
Quick ID: mottled brown with gray, buffy rufous underparts, transverse black bands on head, large round eyes located well back on sides of head, short neck, long bill with prehensile tip, short legs

Length: 10.5" Weight: 3.7 oz Wingspan: 18"

This chunky bird is rarely seen, as the brown mottling on its back makes for exceptional camouflage in thickets where it hides during the day. But when the sun sets, this normally secretive bird becomes the life of the party. On spring nights, the male launches itself into the air in an erratic display to attract the attention of a female.

Sounding a bit like a cartoon character, they produce a nasal buzzy "peent" call. The unusually long bill of the American woodcock is specially designed for probing into the earth to find earthworms. They walk with an unusual back and forth rocking motion. Because their eyes are set far back on their head, these birds can keep an eye on any predators that might sneak up behind them. Another similar bird with a long bill, the common or Wilson's snipe (*Gallinago delicata*), has longer legs and barring on the sides. At dusk in spring, listen for the unusual sound effects of American woodcocks at Jenkins Gap, Loft Mountain area, and Big Meadows.

YELLOW-BILLED CUCKOO
Coccyzus americanus
Cuckoo family (Cuculidae)
Quick ID: long slim body, warm brown above, white underparts, long black tail with large white spots, long decurved bill, lower bill yellow, rufous in wings

Length: 12" Weight: 2.3 oz Wingspan: 18"

A bit larger than a robin, yellow-billed cuckoos have a long tail and hunched over appearance. Often heard rather than seen, these secretive birds have a loud distinctive call that sounds a bit like slow knocking, "ka ka ka ka kow kow kowp." Cuckoos can often be found in areas with tent caterpillars, as this is one of their favorite foods. Listen and look for yellow-billed cuckoos in deciduous woods, including South River Falls, Traces Trail, and Mount Marshall Overlook.

Female ruby-throated hummingbird

RUBY-THROATED HUMMINGBIRD
Archilochus colubris
Hummingbird family (Trochilidae)
Quick ID: iridescent green back and crown, long thin bill; males have a ruby-red throat, females have a white throat

Length: 3.75" Weight: 0.11 oz Wingspan: 4.5"

Unlike many residents of more western states, the only hummingbird that is regularly found in the east is the ruby-throated hummingbird. Because the females lack the ruby-red throat of the male, many people believe these are two different species. Hummingbirds can beat their wings up to seventy-five times per second and zip in and away from their flower nectar source using their ability to fly backwards and hover in midair. Hummingbirds prefer to nectar at orange or red tubular flowers, including wild columbine, cardinal flower, and spotted jewelweed. Lured by sugary nectar, the probing hummingbirds contact the reproductive parts of the plant, either picking up or depositing pollen, thus acting as avian pollinators. Along with Big Meadows, one of the best places to spot "hummers" in the park is at the Old Rag View Overlook.

Northern flicker

RED-BELLIED WOODPECKER
Melanerpes carolinus
Woodpecker family (Picidae)

Quick ID: black and white barred back and wings, white rump, sharp chisel-like black bill, faint reddish belly but looks mostly white; males have red crown and nape, females have a grayish forehead and red nape

Length: 9.25" Weight: 2.2 oz Wingspan: 16"

The zebra-striped back of the red-bellied woodpecker is a better identifying feature than its belly, as the red belly is very faint and often difficult to see. Males have an entirely red crown and nape, while females have a pale forehead with a red patch on the back of the neck. A red-bellied woodpecker has a barb-tipped tongue, which they can stick out 2 inches past the tip of their bill to find insects in trees and under bark. They are sometimes mistakenly referred to as red-headed woodpeckers (*M. erythrocephalus*), but those have an entirely red head and neck and are not frequently seen in the park. A bit larger than the red-belly, the northern flicker (*Colaptes auratus*) is brownish with black barring and has yellow under the wings. Males have a black moustache, which the females lack.

Yellow-bellied sapsucker

They can often be seen foraging on the ground for ants. The smaller yellow-bellied sapsucker (*Sphyrapicus varius*) has indistinct black and white back markings with a bright red patch on the cap, males also have red under the chin. This sapsucker drills horizontal holes in trees to reach the sap.

PILEATED WOODPECKER
Dryocopus pileatus
Woodpecker family (Picidae)

Quick ID: large, black body, white wing patch, white line on neck, large red crest on head; males have a red forehead and a red line behind bill, females have a gray forehead with a black line behind bill

Length: 16.5" Weight: 10 oz Wingspan: 29"

Pileated woodpeckers are year-round residents in Shenandoah. These striking, crow-size birds can be seen throughout the park. As they search for hidden ants, the loud drumming of their bills on tree trunks can be distinctly heard as they carve out rectangular feeding holes. When building a nest cavity, they excavate holes 8 inches wide and from 10 inches to 2 feet deep in dead tree trunks. When observed in their strong and direct flight, pileateds have a distinguishing large white patch in their wings. The word pileated means having a cap, or pileus. Two accepted pronunciations of the word are PILL-ee-ay-tid or PIE-lee-ay-tid. American Indians used the colorful crest of these woodpeckers to adorn their ceremonial pipes. Look for pileateds at Hogwallow Flats Overlook, South River Falls, Mathews Arm, and Mill Prong Trail.

Hairy woodpecker

DOWNY WOODPECKER
Dryobates pubescens
Woodpecker family (Picidae)

Quick ID: small, black wings with white spots, white patch on back, clean white belly, tail black on top, white underneath, white stripes on face; males have red on head, females have black on head

Length: 6.75" Weight: 0.95 oz Wingspan: 12"

Not much larger than a sparrow, downy woodpeckers are commonly seen in the park. They probe under bark and in tall weedy stems such as goldenrod galls for insects, grubs, and larvae. The look-alike hairy woodpecker (*D. villosus*) is much larger than the downy. The bill of the hairy is almost as long as its head, while the downy's bill is about half as long as the depth of its head. Red-bellied woodpeckers (*Melanerpes carolinus*) are larger than the downy and a bit larger than the hairy, and have a zebra-striped back and red on the crown with a gray face. Yellow-bellied sapsuckers (*Sphyrapicus varius*) have indistinct black-and-white back markings. Northern or yellow-shafted flickers (*Colaptes auratus*) are brownish with black barring and yellow under the wings.

Eastern phoebe

EASTERN PHOEBE
Sayornis phoebe
Tyrant Flycatcher family (Tyrannidae)
Quick ID: brownish-gray upperparts with head darker, off-white below

Length: 7" Weight: 0.7 oz Wingspan: 10.5"

Even beginning bird watchers can easily learn this bird's call as it conveniently whistles its name "fee-bee," and it is a frequent sound in spring. One of the earliest birds to return from their migratory home in spring, they quickly begin the mating and breeding process. They are often very familiar, as they frequently build their nests in protected nooks under the eaves of buildings, porches, and overhangs of bridges. They can be seen perched on branches or fences wagging their tails up and down as they wait for an unsuspecting insect to fly by. A few remain here in winter and are often found in low numbers on the annual Christmas Bird Count that includes parts of Shenandoah and the Luray area. A smaller but similar bird in this family, the eastern wood-pewee (*Contopus virens*), also calls its name as well with a slow plaintive "pee-ah-wee."

Eastern wood-pewee

GREAT CRESTED FLYCATCHER
Myiarchus crinitus
Tyrant Flycatcher family (Tyrannidae)
Quick ID: gray back head and chest, yellow belly, rusty tail and wings

Length: 8.75" Weight: 1.2 oz Wingspan: 13"

"Wheep, wheep, wheep," the loud emphatic call notes of the great crested flycatcher alert you to its presence often before you catch sight of this bird. They tend to stay in the canopy at the top of trees snatching insects midair as they fly away. Including the great crested flycatcher, there are ten species of birds in this family found in the park. Eastern wood pewee (*Contopus virens*), Acadian flycatcher (*Empidonax virescens*), and eastern phoebe (*Sayornis phoebe*) are also common breeders here. Look for great crested and other flycatchers at Limberlost, Crescent Rock, Pinnacles Picnic area, and Fox Hollow Trail.

BLUE-HEADED VIREO
Vireo solitarius
Vireo family (Vireonidae)
Quick ID: bluish-gray head, white eye ring with white line to bill, two white wing bars, greenish back, white belly, sides yellowish

Length: 5.5" Weight: 0.56 oz Wingspan: 9.5"

Long known to birders as the solitary vireo, the blue-headed vireo is in the vireo family, which are relatively stocky songbirds with hooked bills. Vireos feed on insects, caterpillars, and berries that they glean from trees and bushes. Unlike warblers that are in constant motion, vireos tend to sit at a perch observing their surroundings. The blue-headed vireo can be distinguished by the white eye ring and white line in front of the eye that resembles a pair of glasses. The red-eyed vireo (*V. olivaceus*) is a very common vireo in Shenandoah with a green back, white breast, and a gray crown with white eye line and red eye. Yellow-throated (*V. flavifrons*) and white-eyed vireos (*V. griseus*) can also be found in the park.

BLUE JAY

Cyanocitta cristata
Crow family (Corvidae)

Quick ID: blue upperparts, blue crest, white marking on wings and tail, grayish-white breast, black necklace; males and females alike

Length: 11" Weight: 3 oz Wingspan: 16"

Along with crows and ravens, blue jays and their western cousins, Steller's jays (*C. stelleri*), are members of the Corvidae family. These two jays are the only ones that sport a pointed crest of feathers on their head that may be raised and lowered at will and are often used to intimidate rivals or predators. Blue jays are excellent mimics, and their calls and sounds can fool even the best birder. Jays sound the crowd alarms, emitting loud calls to alert other birds to nearby predators. They will also engage in mobbing behavior, harassing unwanted birds or even hawks that enter their territory. The eastern bluebird is much smaller and has a rosy breast.

RED-EYED VIREO

Vireo olivaceus
Vireo family (Vireonidae)

Quick ID: olive-green upperparts, white underparts, gray crown, white eyebrow, gray line through eye, adults have red iris while young ones have brown iris, hook on bill tip

Length: 6" Weight: 0.6 oz Wingspan: 10"

Resembling large warblers, vireos have a small hook on the tip of their thick bill, which they use to capture insects. Quite an outgoing bird, the red-eyed vireo whistles a song that sounds like "look-up-way-up-in-the-trees." Having a lot to say, researchers have counted male red-eyed vireos singing more than 20,000 times a day in the spring. A very common bird throughout the park, red-eyed vireos often serenade your visit at picnic areas, including those at Lewis Mountain, Dickey Ridge, and Pinnacles. In fall, red-eyed vireos join the flocks of birds that migrate to the Amazon basin in South America. A great way to help identify birds by their song has been developed by birding experts at the Cornell Lab of Ornithology. This useful app, called "Merlin Bird ID," can be downloaded free. For information, visit merlin.allaboutbirds.org.

COMMON RAVEN
Corvus corax
Crow family (Corvidae)
Quick ID: large, solid black, long narrow wings, wedge-shaped tail, heavy bill; male and female alike

Length: 24" Weight: 2.6 lbs Wingspan: 53"

Ravens are considered by biologists to be one of the most intelligent birds in the world. The raucous "rrronk-rrronk" call of the common raven can be easily heard throughout the park. Ravens are gregarious and perform extraordinary aerial acrobatics, with dives and rolls that rival Olympic gymnasts. They can often be seen from high-altitude overlooks in the park such as Stony Man, Marys Rock, and Old Rag, where they soar effortlessly over the mountaintops. With similar black plumage, crows lack the wedge-shaped tail and heavy bill of the raven. American crows (*C. brachyrhynchos*) and occasionally fish crows (*C. ossifragus*) can be found in the park, but both are much smaller.

BARN SWALLOW
Hirundo rustica
Swallow family (Hirundinidae)
Quick ID: blue-black upperparts, buffy to cinnamon underparts, deeply forked tail with white spots, long pointed wings; male darker than female

Length: 6.75" Weight: 0.67 oz Wingspan: 15"

Zipping through the air over Big Meadows, barn swallows expertly turn and dive, snatching insects in midflight. Their super maneuverability in flight is enhanced by their deeply forked tail, which results in greater aerodynamic lift than that of other swallows. These aerial sprinters have been clocked at up to 35 miles per hour. Found throughout most parts of the temperate world, barn swallows historically nested in caves. Taking advantage of the protection offered by buildings, these and other birds have shifted their nesting sites to under the eaves of buildings or other artificial structures, such as bridges and culverts. Their bowl-shaped nests are formed from mud and grasses that they fasten to a vertical wall under an overhang. In many parts of the world, barn swallows are considered a sign of good luck. It was believed that removal of the nests could cause your cows to stop producing milk or even cause lightning to strike your barn. According to an ancient legend, a barn swallow stole fire from the gods to bring it to humans. This angered the gods into throwing a firebrand at the bird that burned off the inner tail feathers leaving only the outer feathers their original length.

CAROLINA CHICKADEE
Poecile carolinensis
Chickadee and Titmice family (Paridae)
Quick ID: black cap, black throat, white cheek, pale gray below, gray back, gray wings with narrow whitish edging, indistinct edge between white cheek and gray back; male and female look alike

Length: 4.75" Weight: 0.37 oz Wingspan: 7.5"

Carolina chickadees are tiny black-and-white birds with a bold attitude. These fearless small birds are in constant motion, chattering a high-pitched "chick-a-dee-dee-

dee," as they glean insects from leaves and bark. Fiercely protective of their territory, they will attack other birds that invade their space. As omnivores they eat a variety of foods, including insects, seeds, and fruits. The related black-capped chickadees (*P. atricapillus*) sometimes arrive in large numbers when northern winter food sources are not available. Black-caps have lower-pitched call notes. They also sport a bright white "hockey stick" pattern on their wings and a distinct edge between the all-white cheek and gray back. Carolina chickadees are year-round residents, but black-capped chickadees may only be found here in winters when their northern food supplies are limited.

TUFTED TITMOUSE
Baeolophus bicolor
Chickadee and Titmice family (Paridae)
Quick ID: blue-gray back and crest, black forehead, orange sides, white underparts, large black eyes; male and female alike

Length: 6.5" Weight: 0.75 oz Wingspan: 9.75"

Although a common bird in the park, the large-eyed, crested tufted titmouse doesn't stay still very long. In constant motion, it darts quickly from perch to perch, sallying forth with a familiar "peter-peter-peter" song. Dead trees, or snags, in the forest

play a major role in the success and survival of many species, including titmice. Tufted titmice do not excavate their own nest cavities but instead depend on tree holes and cavities vacated by woodpeckers. In winter, titmice are commonly seen at bird feeders in areas outside the park. Another crested bird found in Shenandoah is the cedar waxwing (*Bombycilla cedrorum*). Waxwings are warm brown with gray wings and tail and a distinctive black mask offset by white. Their wings are red-tipped and their tail is yellow-tipped with white undertail feathers.

WHITE-BREASTED NUTHATCH
Sitta carolinensis
Nuthatch family (Sittidae)

Quick ID: blue-gray upperparts, white underparts with inconspicuous rusty patches, whitish face, grayish to blackish cap, sharp pointed bill; males have black cap, females have grayer cap

Length: 5.75" Weight: 0.74 oz Wingspan: 11"

White-breasted nuthatches can often be seen hopping on trees over and around branches—often climbing headfirst down the trunk. As they forage for insects under the bark, they call a deliberate nasal "yank, yank," proclaiming their territory. Nuthatches break open large seeds and nuts by wedging them into cracks in tree bark and hacking at them until they pop open. They also store seeds and insects under pieces of loose bark or under moss or lichens. Nuthatches often forage in loose flocks with chickadees and tufted titmice. The more uncommon red-breasted nuthatches (*S. canadensis*) are smaller and can be recognized by an even more nasal "toy horn" call. Quiet brown creepers (*Certhia americana*) have mottled brown feathers and a long, spiky tail and spiral up trees.

WINTER WREN
Troglodytes hiemalis
Wren family (Troglodytidae)

Quick ID: tiny, brown with black barring, buffy-tan line over eye, normally keeps tiny tail cocked upward; male and female alike

Length: 4" Weight: 0.32 oz Wingspan: 5.5"

Bouncing about like tiny brown ping-pong balls, winter wrens are full of energy and attitude. They spend much of their day in tangled brush searching for insects. Winter wrens prefer cool mountainside or cold-water streams. Winter wrens are the smallest of the three wren species that occur in the park. House wrens (*T. aedon*) have a longer tail and are a lighter brown without the distinct barring of the winter wren. The commonly seen Carolina wren (*Thryothorus ludovicianus*) is stocky with buffy unstreaked underparts and has a white line over the eye. With a constant stream of trills and notes, this tiny sprite has the longest lasting song of Shenandoah's birds. Look for them at Hemlock Springs Overlook at mile 39.7 and Marys Rock Tunnel Overlook at mile 32.2.

CAROLINA WREN
Thryothorus ludovicianus
Wren family (Troglodytidae)
Quick ID: reddish-brown upperparts, buffy underparts, white eyebrow, longish tail, decurved bill

Length: 5.5" Weight: 0.74 oz Wingspan: 7.5"

Bigger than the tiny winter wren, the Carolina wren is much more common and regularly seen and heard in the park. Like bouncing popcorn, these lively and inquisitive birds often hop into the open on shrubs to check out the activities, bobbing their tail up and down. About the size of a chunky but

House wren

small sparrow, these birds are very vocal, calling "teakettle teakettle teakettle" to announce their presence. Carolina wrens don't migrate south for the winter but will often seek food and shelter at lower elevations. They are primarily insectivorous but will also eat seeds and dried fruits in winter. In early mornings, they can be seen hunting for moths attracted to night lights. The smaller house wren (*Troglodytes aedon*) is brown all over and lacks the white eyebrow the Carolina wren sports. To spot these small birds, check around the shrubby edges of picnic areas and campgrounds as well as trails such as Gravel Springs Trail.

GOLDEN-CROWNED KINGLET
Regulus satrapa
Kinglet family (Regulidae)
Quick ID: tiny, olive-gray above, paler off-white below, two dull white wing bars, white eye line, crown patch bordered in black; males have orange crown patches, females have yellow crown patches

Male golden-crowned kinglet crest

Length: 4" Weight: 0.21 oz Wingspan: 7"

Found throughout most of North America, this tiny bird is very familiar to birders. Full of energy, kinglets seem to bounce about the treetops chattering with very high "tsee tsee tsee" notes. Along with its cousin, the ruby-crowned kinglet (*Corthylio calendula*), golden-crowned kinglets often forage in small flocks or with "waves" of warblers, chickadees, titmice, and other birds. When confronted or agitated, males raise their crown feathers to reveal bright orange feathers, while females sport a crown of yellow feathers. Also typically hidden, the crest of the male ruby-crowned kinglet is red, which the female lacks. A good way to tell these two kinglets apart is to look for a white line over the eye of the golden-crowned while the ruby-crowned has a white ring around the eye. Look for these tiny sprites on South River Falls Trail, Hawksbill Trail, Mill Prong Trail, and the Skyland area.

Ruby-crowned kinglet male

Ruby-crowned kinglet female

EASTERN BLUEBIRD
Sialia sialis
Thrush family (Turdidae)
Quick ID: orangish chest and sides, white belly; males have bright blue heads and upperparts, females are dull blue

Length: 7" Weight: 1.1 oz
Wingspan: 13"

Eastern bluebird populations experienced a sharp decline in numbers in the 1960s due to habitat destruction. Concerned

citizens built and set up bluebird boxes, and their efforts have reversed the downward trend; now bluebirds are a common sight in the east. Bluebirds nest in tree trunk cavities where other birds have vacated nesting sites. They prefer nesting sites near open areas such as Big Meadows for easy access to numerous insects. Adult males are bright blue on top with an orangish breast and throat. The females are duller. In the east other birds that are blue include larger blue jays, entirely blue male indigo buntings, and cerulean and black-throated blue warblers, both of which are smaller.

WOOD THRUSH
Hylocichla mustelina
Thrush family (Turdidae)
Quick ID: brown upperparts; cinnamon-brown crown, nape, and upper back; white underparts with extensive coarse dark spots

Length: 7.75" Weight: 1.6 oz
Wingspan: 13"

No musical instrument can compare to the flutelike, melodious song of the wood thrush, which reminds listeners

of the value of national parks such as Shenandoah. Many neotropical migrants such as the wood thrush have recently experienced a rapid decline in numbers, which has been linked to habitat destruction. Fragmentation of the forest has led to increased nest parasitism from the brown-headed cowbird (*Molothrus ater*). In a 1998 study, 75 to 95 percent of all wood thrush nests contained at least one cowbird egg. The veery (*Catharus fuscescens*) is also a common breeder in the park but has less pronounced spots than the wood thrush. You can find wood thrushes at Traces Trail and Milam Gap.

Hermit thrush

VEERY

Catharus fuscescens
Thrush family (Turdidae)

Quick ID: rusty reddish-brown above, buffy belly with reddish-brown spots on the breast; male and female alike

Length: 7" Weight: 1.1 oz Wingspan: 12"

A lyrical inhabitant of forested areas in Shenandoah, the veery sings a lovely downward-spiraling song that enchants listeners on quiet pathways and trails. It forages on the ground, flipping up leaves to find insects. Females and males look alike. Veerys are long-distance migrants that can fly up to 160 miles per night, wintering in central and southern Brazil. The larger brown thrasher (*Toxostoma rufum*) is longer billed, longer tailed, and has thin, dark vertical stripes covering its underparts. The Hermit thrush (*C. guttatus*) is the only thrush you will normally see in North America in the winter, as most thrushes migrate to warmer climates in the tropics. The hermit thrush is identified by its reddish tail that it slowly raises up and down. In winter, look for hermit thrushes at lower elevations where there are cedars and pines.

AMERICAN ROBIN

Turdus migratorius
Thrush family (Turdidae)

Quick ID: upperparts gray to black, breast and underparts reddish-orange, yellow bill; females are often paler than males

Length: 10" Weight: 2.7 oz Wingspan: 17"

The American robin is named for a European robin that is similar in coloration but has been placed in a different family. They sometimes form huge flocks, gleaning food from agricultural fields along with common grackles (*Quiscalus quiscula*), red-winged blackbirds (*Agelaius phoeniceus*), and European starlings (*Sturnus vulgaris*). Robins are found year-round in Virginia, but typically migrate to the relative shelter of the valleys below the park's mountains and other lower elevations in the state in winter.

GRAY CATBIRD
Dumetella carolinensis
Mimic-thrush family (Mimidae)
Quick ID: slate-gray, black cap and tail, rufous
undertail feathers (coverts); male and female alike

Length: 8.5" Weight: 1.3 oz Wingspan: 11"

Gray catbirds are medium-size, dull-gray birds with
a black cap and rusty undertail feathers called
undertail coverts. Their drab coloration helps
camouflage them from predators as they forage for
insects and berries. Catbirds are generally quiet
except for the soft, catlike "meeeurr" call that
gives this species its name. The brown thrasher
(*Toxostoma rufum*) and the northern mockingbird
(*Mimus polyglottos*) are also in the same mimic-
thrush family as catbirds. Brown thrashers are soft
brown with brown streaking on the underparts.
Northern mockingbirds are gray with white in the
wings and tail and white underparts. Catbirds
repeat their call phrases once, brown thrashers
twice, and northern mockingbirds three times.
Habitat loss is causing gray catbird population
numbers to decline in the southeastern United
States. Catbirds can be found throughout the
park especially at the edge of brushy areas below
overlooks and in campgrounds.

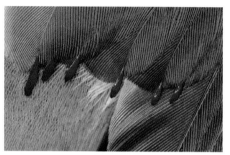

Wing tips

CEDAR WAXWING
Bombycilla cedrorum
Waxwing family (Bombycillidae)
Quick ID: grayish-brown, crest on head, black mask
edged with white, pale yellow on breast and belly,
wings tipped red, yellow band on tail

Length: 7.25" Weight: 1.1 oz Wingspan: 12"

Common throughout in the park, cedar waxwings
often alert you to their presence with a single
noted, thin, high "zeee" call. Social birds, they
typically fly in small flocks and gather at the tops
of trees gleaning fruit and insects before flying
off to another feeding area. The wings are tipped
with red and appear to have been dipped in sealing
wax, which gives these birds their name. Look for
waxwings near fruiting trees such as serviceberries,
cherries, dogwood, and red cedar. You can see
cedar waxwings at Big Meadows, Panorama, Saw
Mill Run Overlook, and Mill Prong Trail.

OVENBIRD
Seiurus aurocapilla
Wood-warbler family (Parulidae)
Quick ID: brownish-olive back, white underparts with rows of black spotty streaks, white eye ring, orange crown patch bordered by dark stripes; male and female look alike

Length: 6" Weight: 0.68 oz Wingspan: 9.5"

The favorite bird of educators, the ovenbird sings its loud rising call of "teacher, teacher, teacher, teacher" throughout eastern forests. More often heard than seen, it tends to stay in shrubby areas foraging on the ground and turning over leaves with its thin bill, searching for insects and snails. The ovenbird gets its name from its unusual ground nest. Weaving together bits of grass, moss, and vegetation, it constructs a woven domed structure shaped like an old-fashioned Dutch oven with a small entrance in the side. When alarmed or agitated, the ovenbird may raise its crest, revealing the orange crown patch. You can remember this bird by thinking that it "scorched its head in the oven." Look for ovenbirds at Crescent Rock, Traces Trail, and Mill Prong Trail.

LOUISIANA WATERTHRUSH
Parkesia motacilla
Wood-warbler family (Parulidae)
Quick ID: brown above, brown stripes on white underparts, white eyebrow stripe, thin bill, pink legs, clear white throat lacking spots

Length: 6" Weight: 0.72 oz Wingspan: 10"

A small bird with a big voice, the Louisiana waterthrush has a loud ringing song that can be heard above the rushing streams it lives by. This water-loving bird methodically bobs its tail up and down as it walks along streams hunting for insects. With its warm brown color and brown streaks, Louisiana waterthrushes only resemble birds in the thrush family. Even though these birds have "thrush" in their name, they are actually members of the unrelated warbler family. Another warbler, the ovenbird, is similarly colored but has a white eye ring rather than the white eyebrow of the Louisiana waterthrush. Look for Louisiana waterthrushes along trails bordering streams such as Dickey Ridge Trail, Graves Mill Trail, and Mill Prong Trail.

Female black-and-white warbler

KENTUCKY WARBLER
Geothlypis formosa
Wood-warbler family (Parulidae)
Quick ID: olive-green back and wings, yellow underparts, black mask with long "whiskers"; females duller

Length: 5.25" Weight: 0.49 oz Wingspan: 8.5"

A warbler of woodland forests, the Kentucky warbler hops about in leaf litter foraging for insects. Its preference for thick cover often makes it hard to spot unless you hear the blurry, rising "chury-churry-churry" call notes that sound a bit like the call of a Carolina wren. Male common yellowthroat warblers (*G. trichas*) have a similar black mask but lack the yellow eyeline. With a characteristic black hood, hooded warblers (*Setophaga citrina*) can also be seen in rich forests throughout the park. Look for Kentucky and other warblers along Snead Farm Trail near Dickey Ridge and Traces Trail at Mathews Arm.

BLACK-AND-WHITE WARBLER
Mniotilta varia
Wood-warbler family (Parulidae)
Quick ID: black and white lengthwise stripes, white stripe over eye, striped crown, slightly decurved bill, two white wing bars; females duller than males

Length: 5.25" Weight: 0.37 oz Wingspan: 8.25"

Like tiny flying zebras flitting through the foliage, black-and-white warblers are instantly recognizable. Like a nuthatch, these striped warblers creep along trees probing under the bark for insects. The only warbler in this genus, *Mniotilta* means "moss-plucking" and refers to the probing activity on trees. Sometimes observed in spring migration, male blackpoll warblers are also black and white but have a solid black head. By fall migration, blackpolls and other colorful warblers lose their bright colors and due to their dull coloration become what are known as "confusing fall warblers." Black-and-white warblers can be seen throughout the park and at South River Falls, Fox Hollow Trail, Pinnacles picnic area, and Bearfence summit.

Common yellowthroat

HOODED WARBLER
Setophaga citrina
Wood-warbler family (Parulidae)

Quick ID: yellow face, olive-green back, yellow underparts, large white spots in tail; male has black hood and bib; female may have faint black hood but lacks black bib

Length: 5.25" Weight: 0.37 oz Wingspan: 7"

Hooded warblers are frequently observed in Shenandoah, and their call can be heard singing from the treetops along many trails and overlooks in the park, including Mill Prong Trail, Graves Mill Trail, Pinnacles Overlook, Limberlost, and Mathews Arm. Male common yellowthroats (*Geothlypis trichas*) are similar, but males have a black mask rather than yellow surrounded by black, and, of course, a yellow throat rather than the black of the hooded warbler. Kentucky warblers (*G. formosa*) have a black mask with yellow over the eye. Black-throated green warblers (*S. virens*) also have yellow in the face but have a black throat.

AMERICAN REDSTART
Setophaga ruticilla
Wood-warbler family (Parulidae)
Quick ID: males are black and orange, females are grayish and yellow

Length: 5.25" Weight: 0.29 oz
Wingspan: 7.75"

One of the most abundant birds in the park, the American redstart is a delight to watch when it fans its brightly colored tail and spreads its wings. This behavior tends to flush insects from hiding—to the delight of this small warbler. The male is velvety black

Female warbler redstart

with Halloween-orange markings. The female is dull gray with yellow markings. The redstart gets its name from the orange-red color in the male's tail; "start" is from the Old English word *steort*, which means "tail." These and other neotropical migrants spend the majority of the year in the tropics and in spring migrate north to Shenandoah to raise their young and enjoy the abundance of insect food sources. Look for the American redstart throughout the park, including near White Oak Canyon Trail, Traces Trail, Beahms Gap, and Beagle Gap.

CERULEAN WARBLER
Setophaga cerulea
Wood-warbler family (Parulidae)
Quick ID: pointed bill, white wing bars, white underneath; males are azure blue with black streaks on back, females are dull greenish-blue

Length: 4.75" Weight: 0.33 oz Wingspan: 7.75"

The vibrant blue cerulean warbler has experienced a serious decline in population due to forest fragmentation, but Shenandoah provides a breeding refuge in its extensive rich forests. Ceruleans migrate to the South American tropics for the winter, where unfortunately many of their home forests have

Female cerulean warbler

been cut down for coffee and other agricultural plantations. Some concerned farmers in the tropics now practice shade-grown coffee methods, which help the environment and provide winter habitat for this species of special concern. Look for ceruleans at Limberlost, South River Falls, and Stony Man Trail.

NORTHERN PARULA
Setophaga americana
Wood-warbler family (Parulidae)
Quick ID: blue-gray back with yellow-olive patch in middle, white underparts, yellow lower bill, two white wing bars; males have bright yellow throat and breast with chestnut band on chest, females have a greenish wash on back and head lack chestnut on chest

Length: 4.5" Weight: 0.3 oz Wingspan: 7"

Warblers are among the smallest bird species, and the northern parula is one of the smallest warblers found in Shenandoah. Even though they may be

Canada warbler

small, these diminutive warblers make up for it with a big, friendly attitude. The rising buzzy insect-like "zeeeeee" trill that drops off abruptly at the end is their trademark call. The name *parula* comes from the word "parus," which refers to another genus of titmouse. Pronunciation of *parula* varies, but most people accent the middle syllable as "par-OOH-la." The similar Canada warbler (*Cardellina canadensis*) also has a gray back and yellow throat, but it has all yellow underparts and sports a black necklace. The Canada warbler also lacks the two white wing bars of the northern parula. Look for these and other warblers along many trails in the park, including Dark Hollow Falls Trail, Mill Prong Trail, and Pocosin Fire Road.

BLACKBURNIAN WARBLER
Setophaga fusca
Wood-warbler family (Parulidae)
Quick ID: males are black and white with bright orange on the face, females are dull black with pale yellow facial patterns

Length: 5" Weight: 0.34 oz Wingspan: 8.5"

With black-and-orange Halloween coloration, the Blackburnian warbler does not stay in the park long enough to celebrate this holiday, heading south in early fall. A prize sighting for birders, the fiery orange face and throat of the adult male fill your binoculars with a delightful picture. Blackburnians are challenging to see because they tend to stay high in treetops foraging for insects. Park biologists are monitoring these and other warblers that historically relied on the giant hemlock forests that have been devastated by the hemlock woolly adelgid since the mid-1980s. You can find Blackburnians and other warblers at Mill Prong Trail, Lewis Mountain picnic area, and Hemlock Springs Overlook.

CHESTNUT-SIDED WARBLER
Setophaga pensylvanica
Wood-warbler family (Parulidae)

Quick ID: black stripes on greenish back, yellow crown on head, yellow wing bars, underparts unstreaked white with chestnut sides toward the front; males have a black mask on face, rich chestnut on sides, females are paler

Length: 5" Weight: 0.34 oz Wingspan: 7.75"

Of the thirty species of warblers that have been observed in Shenandoah, the chestnut-sided warbler is one of the most commonly heard and seen. Preferring to nest along the edges of meadows and thickets, this active warbler darts about the treetops snapping up insects from branch to branch. A neotropical migrant, these

Yellow-rumped warbler

and other warblers breed in Shenandoah during the warm months then head back to their home in the tropics for the winter. Their distinctive song sounds like they are saying "please, please, pleased to meet 'cha" or "see, see, see Miss Beecher." Chestnut-sided warblers can be seen at Limberlost, Dark Hollow Falls Trail, Pocosin Fire Road, and Franklin Cliffs Overlook. Rare in the park during the breeding season, the yellow-rumped warbler (*S. coronate*), also called a Myrtle warbler, was first found breeding in Virginia near Big Meadows Visitor Center.

BLACK-THROATED BLUE WARBLER
Setophaga caerulescens
Wood-warbler family (Parulidae)

Quick ID: males have deep blue above black on face, throat, and sides; white belly; relatively large white wing patch; females have dull greenish, pale stripe above eye, small white wing patch

Length: 5.25" Weight: 0.36 oz Wingspan: 7.75"

A delightful warbler sought after by birders, the male black-throated blue warbler is easy to identify with its deep blue back and head, black throat and sides, and large white wing patch. The

Female black-throated blue warbler

female is dull greenish-blue with a small white patch that resembles a tiny handkerchief. The male and female are so different that they were once thought to be two different species of warblers. The black-throated blue warbler can be seen in the spring and summer in forested areas, gleaning insects in the shady understory. These and other warblers can be seen during fall migration at lower elevations in the park. The genus name has recently been changed from *Dendroica* to *Setophaga* to better represent the uniqueness of this and other related warblers.

EASTERN TOWHEE
Pipilo erythrophthalmus
New World Sparrow family
(Passerellidae)

Quick ID: stocky sparrow, long tail, conical bill, rufous sides, white belly, red eye; males have black head and back, females have brown head and back

Length: 8.5" Weight: 1.4 oz Wingspan: 10.5"

Eastern towhees are often difficult to see but easier to hear. They tend to stay concealed in thick shrubs as they scratch in the underbrush, tossing dead leaves aside as they search for insects. They are easy to identify by their distinctive calls, one that seems to say, "drink your

Female eastern towhee

teeeeee" and the other a "chewink" call note. Until recently the eastern towhee and the closely related spotted towhee (*P. maculatus*) found in western states were considered a single species called the rufous-sided towhee. The eastern towhee lacks the white wing bars and spots on the back of the spotted towhee.

CHIPPING SPARROW
Spizella passerina
New World Sparrow family (Passerellidae)
Quick ID: brown back with black streaks, bright rufous crown, white eyebrow, black eye stripe, grayish unstreaked breast and rump; male and female alike

Length: 5.5" Weight: 0.42 oz Wingspan: 8.5"

Sparrow identification is sometimes a challenge for birders, but by observing subtle details about their markings and habits it can be a fun experience. Chipping sparrows can be identified by their rufous crown and black stipe through the eye with a white "eyebrow." These small sparrows are often seen running on the ground hopping up to feed on grass seeds. Field sparrows (*S. pusilla*) have a pink bill and white eye ring. Seen in winter, American tree sparrows (*S. arborea*) also have a rusty crown but sport a central dark breast spot. Song sparrows (*Melospiza melodia*) are larger with brown stripes overall and a central breast spot. Look for sparrows in fields and open areas, including Big Meadows, Beagle Gap, and Panorama.

SONG SPARROW
Melospiza melodia
New World Sparrow family (Passerellidae)
Quick ID: brown back, heavily streaked breast with large central spot

Length: 6.25" Weight: 0.7 oz Wingspan: 8.25"

One of the most common sparrows in North America, the song sparrow is found in Shenandoah in open fields and meadows such as those found in Beagle Gap and Big Meadows. Their heavy brown streaking helps them remain unnoticed in brushy habitats. The diet of sparrows typically consists of seeds and grains that they crush with their strong bills. White-throated sparrows (*Zonotrichia albicollis*) have a gray breast and a clear white throat with a distinctive yellow spot between the eye and the bill. The call of the white-throated sparrow sounds like it is saying, "Oh sweet Canada, Canada, Canada" while the song sparrow belts out a loud, bright song with three or four notes and then finishes with a complex melodious trill. Some birds, including the song sparrow, have varied dialects depending on their locality.

Field sparrow

White-throated sparrow

DARK-EYED JUNCO
Junco hyemalis
New World sparrow family (Passerellidae)
Quick ID: gray above, white belly, white outer tail feathers, conical bill; males and females similar

Length: 6.25" Weight: 0.67 oz Wingspan: 9.25"

In Virginia dark-eyed juncos are commonly called "snowbirds," as they are typically seen in winter when the snow arrives. However, a different subspecies of junco can be found in Shenandoah National Park. Making the high-elevation mountains of Shenandoah their permanent home, the Appalachian race of the dark-eyed junco entertains warm-weather visitors to the park throughout the year. They hop about trail sides and open areas much like the larger American robin (*Turdus migratorius*), feeding on insects or seeds. They often nest on slopes in well-concealed ground nests. If you can get a close look at their bill, look for the bluish-gray coloration. Migrants from the north join these residents in winter, but they sport pinkish bills.

SCARLET TANAGER
Piranga olivacea
Cardinal family (Cardinalidae)
Quick ID: males have brilliant red, black wings, black tail; females are greenish-yellow with olive-brown wings

Length: 7" Weight: 0.98 oz Wingspan: 11.5"

One of the most popular sightings for birders, spotting a scarlet tanager through the binoculars is always a special treat. The female is dull greenish yellow, which aids in camouflage while nesting. The conspicuous male has scarlet-red plumage with black wings and a black tail. The other red bird that frequents the park is the male northern cardinal (*Cardinalis cardinalis*), which has red wings and a red tail. You may be able to locate scarlet tanagers by listening for their scratchy song that resembles the call of a robin with a cold. They also have a call note that sounds like "chick-purr." Listen for their calls, then watch for the bright flash of red high in the trees. The scarlet tanager and other members of its genus have recently been reclassified from the tanager family to the cardinal family. Look for scarlet tanagers at Gooney Run Overlook, Hogwallow Flats Overlook, Mathews Arm, Stonyman Trail, and Hawksbill.

Female scarlet tanager

Female northern cardinal

NORTHERN CARDINAL
Cardinalis cardinalis
Cardinal family (Cardinalidae)

Quick ID: large orange-red bill, black around bill and crest, long tail; males are bright red, females are buffy-tan with red edging on wings

Length: 8.75" Weight: 1.6 oz Wingspan: 12"

The northern cardinal is so favored over all other Virginia birds that in 1950 it was designated as the official state bird of the commonwealth. Six other states also selected the cardinal to represent them in this official capacity. The color red has long been associated with royalty and worn by officials in many capacities. The Latin name (*Cardinalis cardinalis*) is derived from the red color of the robes of Roman Catholic cardinals. Cardinals have heavy seed-crushing bills that allow them to eat a wide variety of seeds that smaller-billed birds are not able to crack. They also supplement their diet with insects and fruits.

INDIGO BUNTING
Passerina cyanea
Cardinal family (Cardinalidae)
Quick ID: males are deep blue, females are light brown with faint streaking, pale throat

Length: 5.5" Weight: 0.51 oz Wingspan: 8"

Indigo buntings announce their spring arrival back to the park with a loud chorus. Males are often seen perched on treetops or shrubs proclaiming their territory along forest edges, overlooks, and roadsides. They repeat every note twice in doublets—a "here, here, where, where" song. The males are iridescent blue while the females are streaky brown. The streaky dull brown coloration of the females helps to camouflage them from potential predators during nesting season. Along with eastern towhees, indigo buntings can be seen at most overlooks in the park.

ROSE-BREASTED GROSBEAK
Pheucticus ludovicianus
Cardinal family (Cardinalidae)

Quick ID: large, conical, pale bill; males have black head and back, white markings, red triangle on breast, white underparts; females have coarse brown streaking overall, white eyebrow

Length: 8" Weight: 1.6 oz Wingspan: 12.5"

Male rose-breasted grosbeaks are boldly patterned with jet-black feathers interspersed with bright white patches and a crimson-red breast. These birds are highly sought after by birders who are often alerted to their presence by their metallic "chink" call note. Their melodic song sounds somewhat like sneakers squeaking on a gym floor. Female rose-breasted grosbeaks have coarse brown streaking and a white "eyebrow," but lack any striking coloration. Grosbeaks feed on insects, fruits, and seeds, which they crack open with their large heavy bills. During migration they rely heavily on fruits, often staining their bills red and purple from elderberries, mulberries, and poke berries.

Female American goldfinch

AMERICAN GOLDFINCH
Spinus tristis
Finch family (Fringillidae)

Quick ID: short conical bill, short notched tail, white wing bars; male—yellow with black forehead, wings, and tail; female—duller, greenish-yellow

Length: 5" Weight: 0.46 oz Wingspan: 9"

Outside the park American goldfinches are regular visitors to bird feeders along with other small birds such as house finches, Carolina chickadees, and tufted titmice. In the wild they rely on seeds that remain on dried flower heads and weedy plants that have not been cut down or mowed. Shenandoah provides natural spaces for these and other birds that enable them to survive the long cold winters with ample food sources. In the coldest part of winter, they may migrate down the mountainsides to find food. Goldfinches often fly in small flocks and can be recognized by their undulating flight and "potato chip" call. In fall their bright yellow feathers are replaced by dull brownish-yellow plumage resembling that of pine siskins (*S. pinus*).

Eastern American Toad calling

EASTERN AMERICAN TOAD
Anaxyrus americanus
Toad family (Bufonidae)
Quick ID: large, warts with colored spot, variable color from gray to brown to reddish

Length: 2–3.5"

Commonly encountered along moist woodland trails in the park, eastern American toads have stout warty bodies and relatively short legs. The large bulges on their shoulders are parotoid glands that secrete a white fluid used as a defense mechanism against predators. This mild toxin can irritate mucous membranes and cause nausea and may act as a cardiovascular stimulant. Handling toads does not cause warts as once believed, but care should be taken to wash any toxins from your skin. From March to August, the trill of eastern American toads can be heard throughout Virginia, including in the park. Visit the Virginia Herpetological Society website to hear the call of this and other frogs and toads (www.virginiaherpetologicalsociety.com/index.html).

GRAY TREEFROG
Hyla versicolor
Treefrog family (Hylidae)
Quick ID: gray to green (changeable coloration), yellow under hind legs, bumpy skin

Length: 1.3–2"

A tiny frog with a loud voice, the gray treefrog has a melodious trill that adds lyrical background music to warm spring and summer evenings throughout the park. These small frogs have specialized pads on their feet to help them climb about in their tree habitats searching for small insects and invertebrates. They are able to survive the cold temperatures of winter due to glycerol in their blood, which acts as natural antifreeze. Gray treefrogs are often called "rain crows," as people thought they were birds calling from trees, predicting rain. As the humidity rises, treefrogs will often call before, during, and after a summer rain.

PICKEREL FROG
Lithobates palustris
True Frog family (Ranidae)
Quick ID: grayish-tan, double row of irregular-squared dark blotches on back, two prominent ridges on back, yellow to white belly, yellow inner hind legs

Length: 1.8–3"

SPRING PEEPER
Pseudacris crucifer
Treefrog family (Hylidae)
Quick ID: tan, brown, or gray with dark lines forming an X on back, pointed snout

Length: 0.75–1.25"

Although they are only about an inch long, spring peepers can produce a chorus so loud it can be heard over a mile away. Rarely seen, these tiny frogs have a distinguishing X mark on their back. Spring peepers are normally found near wetlands or along the edges of ponds. Another spring singing frog, Upland chorus frogs (*P. feriarum*) can be heard in early spring along Madison Run.

Often found along forested streams and wet areas, pickerel frogs can wander far into meadows, especially in summer. On its back, the two prominent ridges with rows of squarish spots are helpful characteristics to identify the pickerel frog. Toxic skin secretions make it one of the most poisonous frogs in North America; they are toxic to other amphibians and would-be predators. Snakes that normally dine on frogs avoid this species due to the noxious skin secretions. The Latin name was recently changed from *Rana palustris* to *Lithobates palustris*. Their snore-like call has been described as being similar to the lowing of a cow. Listen for their call in the spring from April to May on Fox Hollow Trail. The similar green frog (*L. clamitans*) has a call that resembles banjo strings being plucked.

Upland chorus frog

Green frog

Red eft

WOOD FROG
Lithobates sylvaticus
True Frog family (Ranidae)
Quick ID: tan to rust or dark brown back, black mask through eye, whitish belly

Length: 1.4–2.8"

When the cells of most animals freeze, vital components are lost forever, but the unique physiology of the wood frog allows it to withstand most freezing winter temperatures and thaw back to life in spring. Freezing temperatures initiate an internal response in the frog that creates an accumulation of urea and glycogen, which help protect cells from freezing even though breathing and heartbeats cease. One of the earliest frogs to mate in spring, they rely on temporary ephemeral ponds—called vernal ponds—to lay their eggs. Listen for the hoarse quack sound of wood frogs along the Graves Mill Trail.

RED-SPOTTED (EASTERN) NEWT
Notophthalmus viridescens
Newts and True Salamander family (Salamandridae)
Quick ID: dark red spots outlined in black; aquatic adults are green, terrestrial juveniles are red-orange

Length: 2.25–4.8"

Unique in the salamander world, newts undergo three distinct life cycles. They begin life in freshwater ponds as tadpoles. After 2 to 5 months, they metamorphose into a land stage. During this juvenile stage they leave their watery home and walk into the forest. Now known as red efts, the colorful youngsters can be seen scavenging for invertebrates, especially at night after a rain. Their rough skin contains a powerful neurotoxin called tetrodotoxin, and their bright red-orange coloration serves to warn predators of their toxicity. After 1 to 3 years on land, they return to the water and enter the breeding adult stage as green water-dwelling inhabitants. Newts may live for 12 to 15 years in the wild.

NORTHERN DUSKY SALAMANDER
Desmognathus fuscus
Lungless Salamander family (Plethodontidae)
Quick ID: gray to brownish, light line from eye to angle of jaw, back with brownish stripe bordered by black, creamy belly with black and white speckles, triangular (keeled) tail, hind legs larger than front legs

Northern Dusky Salamander with eggs

Length: 2.5-4.5"

Of the fourteen species of salamanders in Shenandoah National Park, the northern dusky salamander is one of the most commonly found. This species of salamander is found throughout Virginia along shaded streams and wet areas. During the day, they hide under rocks, logs, and debris along streams and waterfalls. At night they emerge to feed on invertebrates such as spiders, slugs, beetles, and worms. Unlike many salamanders, the northern dusky guards its eggs under a rock or other sheltered object until hatched. Predators of these and other salamanders include raccoons, skunks, birds, and water snakes. Northern dusky salamanders are super jumpers and often escape an attack by jumping away. They also have slippery skin and special vertebrae that allow the tail to easily break off when grabbed by a predator. This survival technique leaves the predator with only a wiggling tail while the salamander dashes away. Another tail grows back later. These and other salamanders have traditionally been collected as fishing bait. All wildlife, including salamanders, are protected within the boundaries of Shenandoah National Park.

SEAL SALAMANDER
Desmognathus monticola
Lungless Salamander family (Plethodontidae)
Quick ID: greenish-gray, dark markings, compressed knife-like tail, seal-like head, hind legs larger than front legs

Length: 3.3–5"

The Appalachian Mountains harbor the richest diversity of salamanders in the world. The seal salamander is a robust greenish-gray salamander with dark markings. It can be found in streams and seepage areas, often hiding under rocks or moss. All animals are protected in Shenandoah National Park, but in areas outside the park they are occasionally called "spring lizards" and used as fishing bait, sometimes decimating local populations.

White-spotted slimy salamander

EASTERN RED-BACKED SALAMANDER
Plethodon cinereus
Lungless Salamander family (Plethodontidae)
Quick ID: either striped red back or unstriped lead-colored back lacking the dorsal stripe

Length: 2.25–5"

Hiding by day under rocks, logs, or leaf litter, the eastern red-backed salamander becomes active under the cover of darkness, silently searching the woodland floor for small insects and other small invertebrates. Lizards, which are reptiles, have scales, whereas salamanders are amphibians and have moist glandular skin. Salamanders can drop all or part of their tail to escape the grasp of predators such as birds or raccoons; their tail will later grow back. These salamanders do not always sport a red back, and color variants include a lead-colored back. Another salamander found in the park is the white-spotted slimy salamander (*P. cylindraceus*). This shiny black salamander is spotted with whitish or cream-colored spots. These salamanders could be called "super glue" salamanders, as they secrete a sticky slime that is extremely sticky and very difficult to wash off.

SHENANDOAH SALAMANDER
Plethodon shenandoah
Lungless Salamander family (Plethodontidae)
Quick ID: either red-striped or unstriped, dark
underside with mottling

Length: 3–4.3"

The Shenandoah salamander is endemic to
Shenandoah National Park. Park biologists are
keeping close watch on this federally and state
endangered species to determine its habitat needs
and population numbers. Scientists hypothesize
that the Shenandoah salamander, Peaks of Otter
salamander, and Cheat Mountain salamander all
arose from a common ancestor. As temperatures
gradually rose after the last ice age, this heat-
intolerant ancestor was eventually restricted to a
few disjunct high-elevation, cool mountaintops.
Through time the three populations differentiated
to the three distinct species that remain today. If current rapid climate change continues, the poster child
species of Shenandoah National Park may run out of its cool high-elevation refugia, and there will be
nowhere to go.

NORTHERN RED SALAMANDER
Pseudotriton ruber
Lungless Salamander family (Plethodontidae)
Quick ID: bright orangish red with black scattered spots, black chin, yellowish iris; females are slightly bigger than males

Length: 4-6"

The northern red salamander was designated as the official state salamander of Virginia in 2018. The bright reddish orange color of the northern red salamander resembles the coloration of the poisonous eastern newt, offering some protection from common predators. Indicating toxicity in many animals, bright red colors are known as aposematic coloration. After the first bite, predators typically avoid this toxic meal in the future. When they are threatened, northern red salamanders curl their body, elevating the rear legs and swaying their tail in a wave-like motion from side to side. Northern red salamanders and other members of the Plethodontidae family are lungless salamanders, meaning they lack lungs. Salamanders and other amphibians live part of their lives in water and part on land. After hatching from eggs, the larvae remain in the water and breathe through gills just like fish. After a few years, northern red salamanders undergo metamorphosis and transform into adults, losing their gills and developing legs for walking on land. As adults, northern red salamanders breathe through their skin.

NORTHERN TWO-LINED SALAMANDER
Eurycea bislineata
Lungless Salamander family (Plethodontidae)
Quick ID: yellowish to tan, two dark lines down each side of the body and tail, the broad stripe on back is lighter with dark spots, light yellow belly

Length: 2.5–3.75"

Northern two-lined salamanders are found abundantly in Shenandoah. The northern and southern salamanders were once considered a single species, but the northern two-lined salamander reaches its southern limit in Virginia in Albemarle and Green Counties. Like many salamanders, the northern two-lined salamanders typically stay near wet areas, hiding during the day under logs, rocks, or fallen leaves in forested areas near springs, streams, or seeps. They may wander into the wet forested areas to forage for invertebrates. After laying up to one hundred whitish eggs on the underside of rocks, females guard the eggs until they hatch. Salamanders have a unique defense mechanism to help protect against predators. If attacked, their tails easily disengage and continue to wiggle as the now tailless salamander runs for cover. The salamander doesn't have to worry, its tail will grow back later.

EASTERN BOX TURTLE
Terrapene carolina
Box and Pond Turtle family (Emydidae)
Quick ID: highly domed brown top shell (carapace) with variable yellow markings, head and neck brown with orange to yellow markings, hinged underside (plastron)

Length: shell 4.5–8.5"

Box turtles have a moveable hinge, called a plastron, on the lower part of their shell that allows them to retract inside the shell to avoid predators. The top part of the shell, called the carapace, is high and dome-shaped with bright yellow or orange patterns. They can be found in forests or meadows where they have access to moisture. Box turtles are omnivorous and eat berries, mushrooms, fruits, beetles and other insects, snails, and carrion. The practice of carving initials on a turtle's shell may damage the protective shell and should never be done. In hot weather eastern box (sometimes called woodland box) turtles seek shelter in pools of water or muddy areas. In winter they burrow under leaves, grass clumps, or logs for shelter throughout the cold season.

EASTERN FENCE LIZARD
Sceloporus undulatus
Spiny Lizard family (Phrynosomatidae)
Quick ID: grayish-brown crossband pattern; rough, keeled, pointed overlapping scales; males have bright blue chin and belly

Length: 4–7"

Keep an eye out on the stone walls along Skyline Drive for a scaly gray lizard doing push-ups on warm summer days. Eastern fence lizard males advertise their territory to other males by displaying with push-ups and flashing their bright blue chin and side patches. During mating season in spring, the blue patches are also flashed to attract females. After mating, females lay three to sixteen eggs, and the young lizards hatch in summer and early fall. Fence lizards prey on many types of invertebrates, including beetles, ants, stinkbugs, grasshoppers, spiders, and millipedes.

FIVE-LINED SKINK
Plestiodon fasciatus
Skink family (Scincidae)
Quick ID: brown with 5 light stripes on back; males often have bright orange jaws in breeding season; young skinks have bright blue tail

Length: 5–8.5"

Hikers in Shenandoah will sometimes spy five-lined skinks basking on rocky cliffs such as the quartzite boulders at Blackrock Summit at milepost 84.8. The young have a bright blue tail, but as the skink ages, the blue gradually fades into brown. These reptiles feed on snails and insects, such as spiders, crickets, grasshoppers, and beetles. Skinks possess the ability to break off their tail to elude a predator; they have a fracture plate at the base of the tail that can be separated without significant harm. Within a few months they are able to grow a tail back that is supported by cartilage and usually shorter than the original tail. The uncommon broad-headed skink (*P. laticeps*) is also found in the park but can be twice as long, and males have large expanded orangish jowls.

Broad-headed skink

NORTHERN WATERSNAKE
Nerodia sipedon
Colubrid family (Colubridae)
Quick ID: dark brown with square dark blotches, aquatic

Length: 24–42"

Usually found in or near water, the northern watersnake is often a victim of mistaken identity. Because of its affinity for water, it is often confused with the poisonous cottonmouth or "water moccasin," which is not found in Shenandoah. Watersnakes are found in ponds, streams, rivers, and wetlands in the park. They prey on fish, frogs, crayfish, and small mammals found in or along the edges of waterways. These watersnakes are prey for many predators, including raccoons, snapping turtles, foxes, and other snakes. They defend themselves vigorously when threatened and will bite repeatedly if you try to pick them up. Their saliva contains an anticoagulant that causes profuse bleeding, but they are not poisonous. You can see northern watersnakes in the Camp Rapidan area.

EASTERN GARTERSNAKE
Thamnophis sirtalis
Colubrid family (Colubridae)
Quick ID: olive green to brown, one yellowish-white longitudinal stripe down the back with a lateral stripe on each side, large round eyes with round pupils

Length: 18-26"

The eastern gartersnake holds the honor of being the official state snake of Virginia. The genus name *Thamnophis* comes from the Greek words *thamnos*, which means "bush," and *ophio*, which means "snake." The species name *sirtalis* is Latin and means "like a garter." Gartersnakes are so called either from the striped garters men used to hold up their socks, or from a mispronunciation of the German word for garden. If disturbed these snakes discharge a musk scent from a gland to discourage predators such as hawks, crows, and raccoons. Like any animal, gartersnakes will bite if provoked, but they will typically try to hide or escape the threat. Gartersnakes play an important role in the ecosystem as they prey on rodents, insects, and slugs that damage gardens and crops.

Red-bellied snake

Rough greensnake

NORTHERN RING-NECKED SNAKE
Diadophis punctatus
Colubrid family (Colubridae)
Quick ID: grayish-black, yellow to orange neck ring, yellowish to orange underneath

Length: 10–15"

The aptly named ring-necked snake has a distinctive yellow-to-orange ring around the neck. The neck ring may not form an entire circle but may be broken. When provoked, the ring-necked snake may twist its tail in the air to expose its bright yellowish underparts. The ring-necked snake is one of the most common but secretive snakes in Shenandoah National Park and may be found hiding in rotting logs, leaf litter, or under stones. Active primarily at night they feed on insects, earthworms, and small salamanders. In winter they enter communal dens in sheltered areas. Also, common in the park, the red-bellied snake (*Storeria occipitomaculata*) is similar to the northern ring-necked snake but lacks the neck ring.

SMOOTH GREENSNAKE
Opheodrys vernalis
Colubrid family (Colubridae)
Quick ID: bright green, whitish-cream underside, large round eyes

Length: 12–20"

Greensnakes are slender, bright green snakes that blend in well with grassy meadows and areas with thick green vegetation. The smooth greensnake and the rough greensnake (*O. aestivus*) are both found in the park. The rough greensnake gets its name from its keeled scales; the smooth greensnake lacks these keels, or ridges, on its scales. Greensnakes are not aggressive and rarely bite unless provoked. The smooth greensnake is found in upper elevations in Virginia and seeks shelter in rock piles and under logs. The rough greensnake is slimmer and longer than the smooth greensnake, with average lengths from 22 to 32 inches, and it is more arboreal, spending much of its time in trees, shrubs, and vines. The genus name *Opheodrys* is derived from the Greek words *ophios*, which means "serpent," and *drys*, which means "tree." The species names *aestivus* is Latin for "summer" and *vernalis* means "of springtime."

EASTERN RATSNAKE
Pantherophis alleghaniensis
Colubrid family (Colubridae)
Quick ID: adults are shiny black with whitish chin and neck, checkerboard pattern on belly

Length: 42–72"

The eastern ratsnake, or black ratsnake, is the most commonly seen snake in Virginia. A well-known friend of farmers, the nonpoisonous ratsnake helps keep the population of mice and rodents down in barns and fields. These snakes are excellent

Baby ratsnake emerging from egg

climbers and are able to ascend trees and other vertical objects. They prey on rodents, squirrels, birds, and bird eggs. Commonly called a "pilot snake," this name refers to the folktale that these snakes lead timber rattlesnakes and copperheads to safety when they are in danger. Another folk legend claims that the skin of a ratsnake hung over a fence would bring rain. Due to the blotchy pattern on young ratsnakes, some people erroneously believe that ratsnakes breed with copperheads.

NORTHERN COPPERHEAD
Agkistrodon contortrix
Pit Viper family (Viperidae)
Quick ID: coppery-red, triangular head, hourglass pattern, vertical pupils

Length: 24–36"

One of the two poisonous snakes found in the park, northern copperheads will do their best to avoid human contact and will often freeze in an attempt to camouflage themselves from detection. They have elliptical pupils, and their thick triangular head is the source of the common name "chunkhead." The dark hourglass markings drape the snake like a saddle and are wide on the sides and narrow on the back. Copperhead bites are painful but almost never fatal. Make sure to watch where you step or place your hands, especially when climbing over rocks or logs in the forest. If bitten, seek medical attention as soon as possible. Venom from copperheads and other venomous snakes is currently being tested for use as an anticancer drug.

TIMBER RATTLESNAKE
Crotalus horridus
Pit Viper family (Viperidae)
Quick ID: triangular head, elliptical pupils, yellow phase with dark crossbands, black phase with black head and black marks on dark grayish-brown body

Length: 36–60"

Many people associate rattlesnakes with western states, but the timber rattlesnake is a common resident of Virginia and Shenandoah National Park. Even the Latin name *Crotalus*, which means "rattle," and *horridus*, which means "dreadful," are descriptive of the undeserved reputation that this venomous snake has earned. In late September and early October, timber rattlesnakes head for their communal den sites where they spend the winter, leaving again in April and May. Rattlesnakes are often found on sunny, rocky slopes and ledges. Hikers should take care when climbing over rocks or logs, especially on trails with rock scrambles such as Bearfence Trail. Rattlesnakes rarely bite unless threatened, provoked, or handled. If bitten, remain calm but seek medical attention immediately.

97

AMERICAN EEL
Anguilla rostrata
Freshwater Eel family (Anguillidae)
Quick ID: snake-like fish, gray to greenish-yellow to brownish, long dorsal fin, pointed tail

Length: 2–5' Weight: average 142.08 oz

The snake-like appearance of the American eel and the slimy body causes some anglers to reject this unusual fish, but historically eel was served regularly on the dinner table. Eels have a fascinating life history, beginning life as eggs near the Bahamas in the Sargasso Sea. Their ribbon-like larvae metamorphose as they float on ocean currents until they reach the eastern shore of North America and find their way into freshwater streams such as those in Shenandoah.

MOUNTAIN REDBELLY DACE
Chrosomus oreas
Carp and Minnow family (Cyprinidae)
Quick ID: silver; males also have red, gold, green, black, and yellow; females are duller in color

Length: 1.5–2" Weight: less than 1 oz

One of the most colorful minnows in North America, the mountain redbelly dace, which is found occasionally in the park, is the glamour fish of small mountain streams. Dace are small fish—only about a finger length long—and are often overlooked. The rosyside dace (*Clinostomus funduloides*), the less colorful blacknose dace (*Rhinichthys atratulus*), and the longnose dace (*R. cataractae*) are other minnows that are abundant in the park's waters. Male mountain redbelly dace display their gaudy harlequin coloration only during breeding season.

Rosyside dace

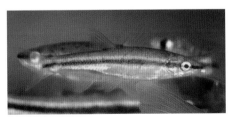

Blacknose dace

FANTAIL DARTER
Etheostoma flabellare
Perch family (Percidae)
Quick ID: drab brown to olive above with faint black bars, whitish below, gold knobs on tips of dorsal spines, tail rounded and prominently tessellated or marbled

Length: 2–3.5" Weight: 1–3 oz

Darters are small, slender fish native to eastern North America. Commonly found in Shenandoah waters, fantail

darters prefer shallow sections of riffles in clear streams. They sit on the stream bottom but quickly dart about when feeding on aquatic insects and worms. Fantail darters lay their eggs on the underside of rocks and cavities where the male aggressively defends the nest until the young hatch.

BLUE RIDGE SCULPIN
Cottus caeruleomentum
Sculpin family (Cottidae)
Quick ID: light-brown flattened body, dark mottling on sides, large mouth and head, large eyes high on head

Length: 3–4" Weight: 0.47–0.65 oz

Advanced techniques in modern genetic analysis have led to major changes in taxonomic status of many organisms, including small freshwater fish called sculpins. The Blue Ridge sculpin is one such fish that in the past was thought to be the same fish as the mottled sculpin (*C. bairdii*). An important

component of the aquatic food chain in Shenandoah, sculpins eat stonefly larvae, which prey upon other small invertebrates. Although uncommon, the Potomac sculpin (*C. girardi*) can also be found in the park.

EASTERN BROOK TROUT
Salvelinus fontinalis
Trout family (Salmonidae)

Quick ID: dark olive-green to brown, cream wavy lines (vermiculations) on back and head, sides with pale spots and red spots with bluish halos, bottom fins white-edged

Length: 5–13" Weight: 2.2–13.2 lbs

Rainbow trout

Drawn by cool mountain temperatures and fast-flowing streams filled with brook trout, President Herbert Hoover chose Rapidan Camp as his summer retreat in 1929. Eastern brook trout are the only trout native to the park; rainbow trout (*Oncorhynchus mykiss*) and brown trout (*Salmo trutta*) have been introduced into park waters. Brook trout require cold water temperatures with sufficient dissolved oxygen. Park fishing regulations include measures to reduce populations of brown trout, which compete with brook trout for

Brown trout

food sources and shelter. Park biologists are also monitoring the effect of increased stream acidity due to acid rainwater, as brook trout are sensitive to changes in water pH. In 1993 the brook trout was designated Virginia's official state fish.

Key Features of Trout in Shenandoah National Park

Trout Species	Description
Rainbow	Small, dense, black spots from tail to top of head with none on gill covers
Brown	Large, dense, black and red spots from tail to head with some on gill covers
Brook	Red spots with blue halos on sides as well as light spots (spots on top side are wavy); fins edged with white

ZEBRA SWALLOWTAIL
Eurytides marcellus
Swallowtail family (Papilionidae)
Quick ID: white with black stripes, long slender tails, red patch on upper hindwings, red stripe on underwings

Wingspan: 2.5–4"

Flight Season: April–October

The unmistakable black-and-white zebra patterns on the wings of the zebra swallowtail make this one of the most easily identifiable of all butterflies in the park. The long thin tails characterize this swallowtail as belonging to a subgroup called kite swallowtails, but all its relatives reside in tropical areas. The host plant for the larvae is another member of mostly tropical plants, the pawpaw (*Asimina triloba*).

APPALACHIAN TIGER SWALLOWTAIL
Papilio appalachiensis
Swallowtail family (Papilionidae)
Quick ID: pale yellow with black markings, slight blue on wing edges

Wingspan: 3.4–4.5"

Flight Season: April–June

Very similar to the familiar eastern tiger swallowtail (*P. glaucus*), the Appalachian tiger swallowtail is larger and only flies from April through June. Readily seen in Shenandoah, it glides through forested areas more often than the eastern tiger swallowtail, which prefers open country. The larvae feed on the leaves of black cherry.

Appalachian tiger swallowtail underwing

EASTERN TIGER SWALLOWTAIL
Papilio glaucus
Swallowtail family (Papilionidae)
Quick ID: males are yellow, females are yellow or black, both have vertical black stripes, blue and orange markings on hindwings, long tails, slow flight

Wingspan: 2.5–4.5"

Flight Season: March–October

Designated as the official state insect of Virginia, this lovely swallowtail graces the license plates of Virginia butterfly lovers. The large yellow tiger-striped wings of the eastern tiger swallowtail are easily

Female dark form

identifiable markings for this common butterfly. At least it is easy until you learn that the female may also be black rather than yellow. The coloration of the black females provides them some protection from predators, as they mimic pipevine swallowtails, which are distastefully toxic to potential predators. You can often notice faint shadows of dark stripes on the black females. This swallowtail nectars on many flowers, including milkweed, bee balm, lilies, phlox, and joe-pye weed. Food plants for the caterpillars include black cherry and tulip tree.

Spicebush swallowtail caterpillar

SPICEBUSH SWALLOWTAIL
Papilio troilus
Swallowtail family (Papilionidae)
Quick ID: black with white marginal spots, upper hindwing dusty blue, underside hindwing with two rows of orange spots

Wingspan: 3–4"

Flight Season: April–September

Some insects have developed a critical relationship with particular plants and are dependent on them for a successful life cycle. The spicebush swallowtail is named for one of the caterpillar's food plants, spicebush (*Lindera benzoin*). The caterpillars can also be found on small sassafras trees (*Sassafras albidum*). Even though spicebush swallowtails are fair game for potential predators, such as birds, they have a very similar coloration to that of the poisonous pipevine swallowtail (*Battus philenor*), which contains distasteful, toxic alkaloids. As caterpillars, the pipevine swallowtails eat the leaves of pipevines (*Aristolochia*), including Dutchman's pipe (*A. macrohylla*) and Virginia snakeroot (*A. serpentaria*), which contain aristolochic acid.

Pipevine swallowtail

ORANGE SULPHUR
Colias eurytheme
White and Sulphur family (Pieridae)
Quick ID: underside yellow, upper side orange with black margin

Wingspan: 1.4–2.7"

Flight Season: March–October

The medium-size orange sulphur is a common butterfly seen in waysides and meadows along Skyline Drive. The similar clouded sulphur (*C. philodice*) is slightly larger and has no orange on the wings. These sulphurs seek out members of the pea family as larval host plants, including clovers and alfalfa. Other similar butterflies that may be found in the park are the cloudless sulphur (*Phoebis sennae*) and sleepy orange (*Abaeis nicippe*). Look for orange sulphurs at overlooks in the park, including Old Rag View Overlook and Timber Hollow Overlook.

WEST VIRGINIA WHITE
Pieris virginiensis
White and Sulphur family (Pieridae)
Quick ID: soft white papery wings, faint grayish-brown scaling on veins, body black on top

Wingspan: 1.2–1.6"

Flight Season: April–May

When the first spring flowers are popping open, the West Virginia white may be seen meandering in slow delicate flight in wooded areas, nectaring on spring beauty, violets, and other early bloomers. They are dependent on cut-leaved toothwort (*Cardamine concatenate*), as the caterpillars need to eat from this plant to survive. Unfortunately, the females will readily lay their eggs on the invasive garlic mustard (*Alliaria petiolata*), and those ill-fated developing caterpillars do not survive. Park botanists have implemented measures to reduce the number of the nonnative garlic mustard plants. The ubiquitous cabbage whites (*P. rapae*) are smaller and usually have black spots on the wings. The smaller falcate orangetip (*Anthocharis midea*) female has checkered wing edges, and the male has orange-tipped wings.

CABBAGE WHITE
Pieris rapae
White and Sulphur family (Pieridae)
Quick ID: white to yellowish-white, forewing with black tip; females have one black spot on the wings while males have two black spots

Wingspan: 1.2–1.7"

Flight Season: March–November

Thriving in most of North America, the cabbage white butterfly nectars of a wide variety of plants, including mustards, dandelion, clovers, asters, and mints. Native to Asia, Europe, and North Africa, this butterfly was introduced to the United States in the 1800s. The caterpillars of the cabbage white butterfly cause significant crop damage and are considered a detrimental pest. The small green caterpillars with thin yellow racing stripes often gnaw away on neat rows of cabbage, broccoli, and radishes. This sight sent gardeners running for an old coffee can with a bit of kerosene in the bottom to drop the ravenous caterpillars in. Look for these naturalized butterflies in most open areas of the park, including the Skyland area near Massanutten lodge and all overlooks, including Spitler Knoll Overlook and Naked Creek Overlook. A similar white native butterfly, the falcate orangetip

Cabbage white underwings

Female falcate orangetip

(*Anthocharis midea*), is similar to the cabbage white but is more heavily marbled below and the males have bright orange wingtips.

APPALACHIAN AZURE

Celastrina neglectamajor
Gossamer-wing family (Lycaenidae)
Quick ID: upperwings light blue to violet-blue, underwings chalky blue with pale markings

Wingspan: 1.1–1.4"

Flight Season: May–June

The Appalachian azure is the largest of the similar-looking blue butterflies that have different flight times in this area. Other similar butterflies are the spring azure (*C. ladon*) and the summer azure (*C. neglecta*). Look for Appalachian azure butterflies on black cohosh plants, where they deposit their eggs on the young flower buds. You can see the caterpillars being tended by ants on black cohosh at Crescent Rocks Overlook in July.

EASTERN TAILED-BLUE

Cupido comyntas
Gossamer-wing family (Lycaenidae)
Quick ID: hindwings with tails, underwing silvery gray with several small orange spots on hindwing; males are bright blue above, females are dark bluish-gray above

Wingspan: 0.75–1"

Flight Season: April–October

The eastern tailed-blue is abundant throughout the eastern United States. From April through October in Shenandoah, it can be found in woodland clearings, fields, and meadows. Other similar small blue butterflies lack the threadlike hindwing tails. The adults nectar at ground-hugging flowers, such as clovers and wild strawberry as well as asters and cinquefoils. The caterpillars feed on plants in the pea family, including clovers, vetches, and bush clovers.

BROWN ELFIN
Callophrys augustinus
Gossamer-wing family (Lycaenidae)
Quick ID: upperside of male is grayish-brown, upperside of female is reddish brown, undersides of both are chestnut brown with dark irregular line, hindwing darker at base, tailless

Wingspan: 1-1.2"

Flight Season: March–April

Brown elfins are the most common elfin in Shenandoah, but they require a very specific dry, acidic environment where heath plants grow. Often knowing the host plant and where it grows is a great way to find the butterflies who are picky eaters. Adults nectar from the flowers of blueberry, spicebush, serviceberry, mountain laurel, and willows. The adult lays eggs on heath plants, such as blueberry, and the bright green caterpillars enjoy the nutritious leaves. Two other elfins can occasionally be seen in the park, the Henry's elfin (*C. henrici*) and eastern pine elfin (*C. niphon*). Henry's elfin larvae feed on redbud, and pine elfin larvae feed on pine needles. Two other elfins are potentials for the park so keep an eye out for frosted elfins (*C. irus*) and hoary elfins (*C. polios*). Hoary elfin caterpillar feed on bearberry and trailing arbutus. Bearberry grows at Miller's Head Trail, and trailing arbutus can be found along trails especially in the southern section. Frosted elfin larvae feed on flowers in the pea family, including lupines such as those that grow along Madison Run Trail.

EARLY HAIRSTREAK
Erora laeta
Gossamer-wing family (Lycaenidae)
Quick ID: underside pale green with bright orange spots, upper side iridescent blue and black

Wingspan: 0.75–1"

Flight Season: April–September

Rarely seen, the early hairstreak is a treat for butterfly enthusiasts. These special small butterflies descend from their canopy perches to nectar on fleabane, daisies, and milkweed. The larvae feed on the nut tissue of American beech and beaked hazelnut. The rare butterfly has been seen at high elevations in Shenandoah.

AMERICAN COPPER
Lycaena phlaeas
Gossamer-wing family (Lycaenidae)

Quick ID: upper wing orange-red with black spots, hindwing gray with orange-red outer margin, underside gray with orange zigzag on hindwing

Wingspan: 0.9–1.4"

Flight Season: June–September

The American copper has an eye-catching bright orange pattern and is a treat for butterfly watchers. This medium-size butterfly tends to fly fairly close to the ground, aggressively defending its territory from other butterflies and insects. Found in meadows and fields and roadsides, they nectar on a variety of flowers. Docks and sheep sorrel are the food plants of the larvae. Look for these and other butterflies in Big Meadows.

Monarch caterpillar

MONARCH
Danaus plexippus
Brushfoot family (Nymphalidae)
Quick ID: orange with black veins, white spots on black wing borders

Wingspan: 3.5–4"

Flight Season: April–November

One of the most well-known and beloved of all members of the insect world, the monarch easily lives up to its celebrity status. The natural history story of this large orange butterfly has ignited the spark of interest in many young people that has carried them into a lifetime study of nature. The yellow-and-black-striped caterpillars feed on plants in the milkweed family, ingesting toxins that linger into adulthood and render them distasteful to predators. The butterfly's orange-and-black warning coloration is recognized by predators and confers parallel protection to other similarly colored butterflies, such as viceroys. In late September, monarchs migrate by the thousands to Mexico where they overwinter before their offspring make the long journey back. These late season individuals are stronger with tougher wings to make the long migration. Look for monarchs and many other butterflies in Big Meadows and Old Rag Overlook.

COMMON BUCKEYE
Junonia coenia
Brushfoot family (Nymphalidae)
Quick ID: brown, large eyespots, orange bands on forewing

Wingspan: 1.5–2.7"

Flight Season: March–November

The distinctive large eyespots on the common buckeye make it very easy to recognize. The eyespots are used as a defense mechanism to frighten away predators such as birds. Buckeyes nectar on asters, chicory, knapweed, and a variety of other flowers. They lay their eggs on the underside of larval host plant leaves, such as toadflax and plantain. In spring the caterpillars feed on the foliage, flowers, and fruits of these host plants.

RED-SPOTTED PURPLE
Limenitis arthemis astyanax
Brushfoot family (Nymphalidae)
Quick ID: black with iridescent blue on upperwings, row of red-orange spots on underwing

Wingspan: 2.25–3.5"

Flight Season: April–October

The red-spotted purple has a similar color to that of the poisonous pipevine swallowtail (*Battus philenor*), thus providing it some protection from predators. This kind of mimicry is known as Batesian mimicry. The North American Butterfly Association (NABA) now considers the red-spotted purple and the white admiral (*L. a. arthemis*)—long considered separate species—two races of the same species. The white admiral has a broad white band across its wings and a more northern distribution than the red-spotted purple. The new designation for the two races is red-spotted admiral.

MOURNING CLOAK
Nymphalis antiopa
Brushfoot family (Nymphalidae)
Quick ID: upper side purplish-black bordered by a broad yellow band and blue spots, underside dark brown with dark striations

Wingspan: 3–4"

Flight Season: May–October

Gracefully gliding through the crisp spring air, the mourning cloak is a beautiful and much appreciated harbinger of spring. A broad irregular yellow border and a row of bright blue spots complement the velvety purplish-black wings of this butterfly. They overwinter in sheltered crevices and may come out of hibernation on warm winter days to feed on running sap and decaying matter.

PEARL CRESCENT
Phyciodes tharos
Brushfoot family (Nymphalidae)
Quick ID: orange with variable dark bands and markings

Wingspan: 1.25–1.6"

Flight Season: March–November

The pearl crescent has the same orange coloration as the well-known monarch but is much smaller. It is also very similar to, but again smaller than, the medium-size meadow fritillary (*Boloria bellona*). Common in open areas, it nectars on a variety of flat-topped flowers, including asters, goldenrods, yarrow, and dandelions.

BALTIMORE CHECKERSPOT
Euphydryas phaeton
Brushfoot family (Nymphalidae)
Quick ID: black with red-orange crescents on outer margins of wings, rows of creamy white spots inward on the wings

Wingspan: 1.7–2.7"

Flight Season: May–June

The striking colors of the Baltimore checkerspot are sure to draw attention from anyone spotting this beauty, including predatory birds. Any bird that tries to take a nibble of this butterfly, however, soon learns that they are not tasty morsels! They contain iridoid compounds derived from their host plants. Depending on a specific plant, the Baltimore checkerspot larva feed only on turtlehead flowers for their livelihoods. Since turtleheads only grow in wet, marshy areas, this is where you will find the Baltimore Checkerspot. This spectacular butterfly is not commonly seen in the park, but keep your eyes open in the Big Meadows area or wherever you find turtlehead. The black, orange, and white coloration of this butterfly is replicated on the flag of Maryland . . . which came first?

GRAY COMMA
Polygonia progne
Brushfoot family (Nymphalidae)
Quick ID: upper side tawny orange-brown with dark border, underside dark gray with fine lines, light grayish patch on underside forewing

Wingspan: 2.1–2.4"

Flight Season: June–October

Also known as anglewings, commas are named for a silvery mark on their hindwing that resembles a comma. They have sharply angled wings and look like dead leaves when their wings are closed. The gray comma, more typical of cool Canadian zones or boreal forests, is found at higher elevations in the park. They feed on rotting fruit, carrion, dung, and tree sap. Other members of this genus frequently encountered in the park are the eastern comma (*P. comma*) and question mark (*P. interrogationis*).

Question mark

Eastern comma

Question mark underwing

Eastern comma underwing

GREAT SPANGLED FRITILLARY
Speyeria cybele
Brushfoot family (Nymphalidae)
Quick ID: large, orange with black markings, underwing with silver markings

Wingspan: 2.9–4"

Flight Season: May–October

One of the most widespread fritillaries in the east, the great spangled fritillary brightly decorates meadows and wildflower-filled fields in the park. The caterpillars are black with rows of orange and black spines. As caterpillars they feed on various violets along woodland paths; as larvae they overwinter near violets and feed on the plant in spring. The smaller variegated fritillary (*Euptoieta claudia*) and the even smaller meadow fritillary (*Boloria bellona*) lack the silvery markings on the underwings.

Variegated fritillary

American lady underwing

AMERICAN LADY
Vanessa virginiensis
Brushfoot family (Nymphalidae)
Quick ID: upperparts orange with dark markings and small white spots near front edge, two eyespots on underside of hindwing

Wingspan: 1.75–2.4"

Flight Season: April–October

A very common and pretty butterfly, the American lady is orange with dark markings and two "eyespots" on the underside of the hindwing. The very similar painted lady (*V. cardui*) has four small eyespots on the hindwing's

Painted lady

underside. With an erratic flight, these butterflies nectar at a variety of flowers, including milkweeds, dogbanes, asters, goldenrods, and sunflowers. Caterpillar host plants include pussytoes, burdock, and ironweed. The intricate underside of the red admiral (*V. atalanta*) is similar to that of American and painted ladies but is primarily black with an orange stripe on its upper wing.

Red admiral

Red admiral underwing

Caterpillar

SILVER-SPOTTED SKIPPER
Epargyreus clarus
Skipper family (Hesperiidae)
Quick ID: brown, lobed hindwing, gold spots on forewing, silvery-white blotch on underside of hindwing

Wingspan: 1.75–2.4"

Flight Season: March–October

Most skippers are considered challenging for butterfly watchers to identify, but the silver-spotted skipper is conspicuous. It is larger than most skippers in this area, and the large silvery-white patch on the underside of its hindwing is a helpful field mark to look for when identifying this brown butterfly. In the park, look for these butterflies nectaring at many types of flowers. You may find the striking caterpillar on young black locust, which often grows along Skyline Drive. On the annual Fourth of July Butterfly Counts in the park, the silver-spotted skipper numbers are often in the hundreds to over 1,000 seen in one day.

WILD INDIGO DUSKYWING
Erynnis baptisiae
Skipper family (Hesperiidae)
Quick ID: dark brown to black with small transparent whitish patches and spots, grayish brown fringe on wings

Wingspan: 1.3–1.7"

Flight Season: April–August

Often seen just steps ahead of hikers on open trails, the wild indigo duskywing is a common butterfly in Shenandoah. Historically this butterfly was uncommon in the park but with the spread of crown vetch it has become plentiful. The wild indigo duskywing is found in eastern states from New England to northern Florida. Caterpillars eat wild indigo and crown vetch. Adults nectar from the flowers of blackberry, clover, black-eyed Susan, wild strawberry, and dogbane. Other similar dark butterflies include Horace's (*E. horatius*), which is active spring through fall. Duskywings seen only in spring are dreamy (*E. icelus*), Juvenal's (*E. juvenalis*), and sleepy (*E. brizo*). Late in the day, duskywings will often wrap their wings around a twig and cryptically disappear from would-be predators.

SACHEM
Atalopedes campestris
Skipper family (Hesperiidae)
Quick ID: variable dull yellowish-orange with
brownish-black markings

Wingspan: 1.2–1.6"

Flight Season: May–November

Sachems are members of a family of butterflies
called skippers. With over 280 species in North
America, they are widespread but often quite
challenging to identify. Of the over twenty species
of skippers in Shenandoah, the sachem is one
of the most commonly seen. Sachems and other
skippers generally sit with their wings closed
or partially open. Many skippers, including the

Indian skipper

sachem, have what appear to be double wings with one inner set and one outer set, somewhat like a W.
Sachem caterpillars feed on grasses. Adults nectar from many flowers, including milkweed, dogbane,
clover, thistles, asters, and ironweed. They are typically found in disturbed, open areas and meadows.
Animated flyers, these butterflies often perform aerial combative territorial displays with invaders. The
similar Indian skipper (*Hesperia sassacus*) is less frequently seen in Shenandoah.

ZABULON SKIPPER
Poanes zabulon
Skipper family (Hesperiidae)
Quick ID: dark markings; males have bright orange above and yellow below, females are dull brown with white edge at top of hindwing

Wingspan: 1–1.4"

Flight Season: May–September

Skippers make up about one-third of all the butterfly species in North America. Skippers are typically small to medium size and brown with various yellowish or dark markings. They have stout bodies, six legs, and

Male Zabulon skipper

large heads and eyes. Bright yellowish male Zabulon skippers are similar to the related Hobomok skipper (*P. hobomok*), while the female is similar to the dull brown clouded skipper (*Lerema accius*). Other similar skippers found in the park include Peck's, Indian, fiery, and sachem.

CTENUCHA MOTH
Ctenucha virginica
Erebid Moth family (Erebidae)
Quick ID: metallic blue, head and sides of neck orange, fringes on wings, forewing grayish-brown with metallic blue at base, hindwing black; males have feathery antennae

Wingspan: 1.5–1.9"

Flight Season: May–July

Most moths are nocturnal, but the brightly colored ctenucha moth (pronounced ten-OOCH-ah) also flies during the day. The striking metallic blue coloration is very noticeable as the moth nectars on a variety of flowers, including goldenrods and goats beard. The caterpillars, which are yellow and white with black bristles, feed on grasses, sedges, and irises. More commonly found in northern United States and Canada, the ctenucha moth reaches its southern boundary in Virginia. Big Meadows is a great place to search for these unusual beauties. The similar grapeleaf skeletonizer moth (*Harrisina americana*) is a pest that defoliated grapes and Virginia creeper leaves. Members of this family produce hydrogen cyanide, which acts as a toxin to deter predators.

AZALEA CATERPILLAR
Datana major
Prominent Moth family (Notodontidae)
Quick ID: black with eight broken, yellow, lengthwise stripes; head, legs, and last segment red; fine hairs cover body

Length: 2"

Colorful caterpillars with an interesting defense behavior, azalea caterpillars are the larval stage of the major datana moth, which is a nondescript tannish-brown moth with a wingspan of 1.6 to 2.0 inches. The caterpillars are very colorful and noticeable as they munch on azaleas or blueberries. Look for them in Big Meadows in August and September chowing down on low shrub leaves. If disturbed, in an effort to startle a would-be predator, they rapidly arch their backs revealing the red legs before dropping to the ground.

Grapeleaf skeletonizer

Giant leopard moth caterpillar

MILKWEED TUSSOCK CATERPILLAR
Euchaetes egle
Erebid Moth family (Erebidae)
Quick ID: adults are mousy gray with yellow abdomen; larva are gray to black with bristly tufts of black, white, and orange hairs

Wingspan: 1.2–1.6"

Flight Season: May–September

Even though the dull gray-brown adult is unremarkable, the milkweed tussock, or milkweed tiger moth, caterpillar is striking. With a black body blanketed in orange, black, or white bristly tufts, the caterpillars are easy to spot. They feed on the leaves of milkweeds and dogbanes, and like other larvae that feed on milkweeds, the caterpillars gain chemical defenses from the toxic cardiac glycosides in the plant, which are passed on to the adults making them distasteful to predators such as bats. Monarch caterpillars prefer to feed on young milkweed leaves, while the milkweed tussock caterpillars often feed on older milkweeds. They avoid the sticky latex in the leaves' veins by skeletonizing the leaves, leaving only the veins.

GIANT LEOPARD MOTH
Hypercompe scribonia
Erebid Moth family (Erebidae)
Quick ID: adults are large, white with black circular spots; larva have shiny black bristles with red bands between body segments

Wingspan: 2.2–3.5"

Flight Season: April–September

Sharing the same camouflaging spots as a leopard, the giant leopard moth, also known as the great leopard moth, is distinctive among its night-flying relatives. The males are often attracted to lights at night. The caterpillars somewhat resemble the familiar woolly bear (*Pyrrharctia isabella*) caterpillars. When they curl up in a defensive ball, you can easily see the bright red warning coloration bands that identify this caterpillar. When handled, some bristly caterpillars can release a toxin that can cause allergic reactions, but the bristles of this caterpillar are harmless to humans.

GYPSY MOTH
Lymantria dispar
Erebid Moth family (Erebidae)
Quick ID: males are yellowish-brown with black markings, feathery antennae; females are larger, ivory white with faint jagged lines and black markings

Total Length: 1–1.2"

Flight Season: July (females flightless)

The gypsy moth was introduced from Europe into Massachusetts in 1869 for use in the development of a silkworm business. Unfortunately, the larvae have insatiable appetites and consume the leaves of over 300 species of plants—with devastating results. Gypsy moths reached Shenandoah National Park in 1984, and from 1987 to 1995 extensive defoliation of oaks resulted. This repeated defoliation (often with drought) caused moderate to heavy oak mortality in some areas of the park. The defoliation of oaks affects acorn production, which plays a major role in the sustainability of many forest inhabitants, including squirrels, deer, turkeys, and black bears.

LUNA MOTH
Actias luna
Saturniid Moth family (Saturniidae)
Quick ID: very large, lime-green, long twisted tails, elliptical eyespots

Wingspan: 3–4.1"

Flight Season: April–August

Unmistakable even at night, luna moths are very large and are attracted to lights around buildings and parking lots. They rest during the day on trees with their wings flattened rather than held upright like most moths. After emerging from their cocoons, adults only live about one week. During this week they do not eat; their prime objective is to find a mate. The caterpillars feed on cherry trees, hickories, walnuts, and sumac as well as other plants.

ROSY MAPLE MOTH
Dryocampa rubicunda
Saturniid Moth family (Saturniidae)
Quick ID: pastel pink and yellow, hairy yellow head

Wingspan: 1.3–2"

Flight Season: April–September

Even for people who are not moth fans, the pink and yellow coloration of the rosy maple moth is a spectacular find. Moths in the Saturniidae family are some of the most spectacular insects in the world, with large sizes and colorful wing patterns. Rosy maple caterpillars feed on a variety of maples.

HUMMINGBIRD CLEARWING MOTH
Hemaris thysbe
Sphinx Moth family (Sphingidae)
Quick ID: golden-olive back, yellow belly, dark burgundy abdomen, wings mostly clear with dark reddish borders

Total Length: 1–1.2"

Flight Season: March–October

The hummingbird clearwing moth is aptly named, as its appearance and behavior often cause it to be mistaken for a small hummingbird. The moths have a long, coiled mouthpart called a proboscis that they uncoil to dip into a flower to sip nectar. Active during the day, they prefer tubular flowers such as honeysuckles, thistles, and monarda. The snowberry clearwing moth (*H. diffinis*) mimics bumblebees and can be seen in Big Meadows nectaring at flowers.

Snowberry clearwing moth

123

Common garden spider

MARBLED ORB WEAVER
Araneus marmoreus
Orb-weaver family (Araneidae)
Quick ID: large, orange to pale yellowish body; orange-, white-, and black–banded legs
Length: 3.1"

Because of its round, bright orange body, the marbled orb weaver is sometimes dubbed the pumpkin spider or Halloween spider. Orb-weaver spiders build large wheel-shaped webs at dusk and wait at the edge for prey to become trapped in the silken net. They typically rebuild their web each day. Another commonly seen orb weaver is the black and yellow argiope (*Argiope aurantia*), or common garden spider.

ARROWSHAPED MICRATHENA
Micrathena sagittata
Orb-weaver family (Araneidae)

Quick ID: reddish-brown edged in yellow, arrow-shaped abdomen with black depressions, variable red and black patterns below, legs reddish-brown; females have spines on abdomen

Length: males are 0.20", females are 0.35"

Orb weavers build spiral webs with wagon-wheel spokes of silken threads. The spider sits in wait for insects such as leaf hoppers and flies to

become ensnared in the sticky web before pouncing on the prey. The female has intimidating spines on the rear; the male lacks these large spines. The scientific name *Micrathena* is a combination of the Greek word for "small" and Athena, the Greek goddess who wore armor and was also a weaver. The species name *sagittata* is Latin for "arrowed."

DARING JUMPING SPIDER
Phidippus audax
Jumping Spider family (Salticidae)
Quick ID: black with tiny whitish hairs, eight black eyes, bright green iridescent mouthparts (chelicerae)

Length: 0.51–0.78"

Fascinating and amazingly successful little creatures, daring jumping spiders are perhaps first noticed running quickly across flat surfaces as they actively hunt for suitable prey. They can jump ten to fifty times their own body length to tackle prey or escape enemies. Harmless to humans, their iridescent mouthparts, called chelicerae, are used to grasp their prey and inject venom. Jumping spiders have the sharpest vision of all spiders and follow their prey intently with their eight eyes. They do not build webs, but instead use their silk to make shelters where they sleep each night, then use the silken shelters to spend the winter in a state of dormancy.

WHITE-BANDED CRAB SPIDER
Misumenoides formosipes
Crab Spider family (Thomisidae)
Quick ID: abdomen widest at rear, white line through eyes; male—shiny red, yellow, or green; female—yellow, white, or light brown

Length: males are 2.5–4", females are 0.19–0.47"

Sometimes called flower crab spiders, the white-banded crab spider sits motionless on flowers waiting for passing insects, such as bees, wasps, or flies. With their front legs outstretched, they resemble tiny crabs amid the white or yellow flower heads. They are one of the few spider species capable of changing colors depending on the flower where they are perched. The color change is not instantaneous but takes several days. The very similar goldenrod crab spider (*Misumena vatia*) lacks the white band below the eyes.

Crab spider and clouded skipper

Goldenrod crab spider

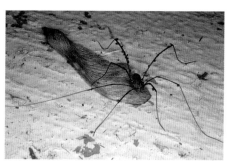

DADDY LONG LEGS
Leiobunum spp.
Harvestman family (Sclerosomatidae)
Quick ID: flat rounded unsegmented body; variable brown; eight very long, bent, spindly legs
Length: 3.5"

A very common myth has followed the daddy long legs claiming it is one of the most venomous spiders in the world. Folklore and myths are readily passed on through generations. In one survey of our local college class, 95 percent of respondents believed these harmless daddy long legs were extremely venomous. Much misaligned, this gentle giant is totally harmless to humans. Also called grandaddy long legs or harvestmen, they resemble giant spiders, but they are more closely related to scorpions than spiders. Their mouth lacks fangs and is so tiny they can only eat small insects and worms that they sense with their second pair of legs. Unlike spiders, they do not build webs, and are not venomous at all. They also lack stingers. Another myth surrounding the daddy long legs is if you kill one it will rain the next day, ruining your plans. Farmers in Europe believed if you held a daddy long legs by all legs except one, the free leg would point you in the direction of your lost cattle. Red mites sometimes parasitize daddy long legs.

BLACK WIDOW SPIDER
Latrodectus mactans
Cobweb Spider family (Theridiidae)
Quick ID: females are shiny patent-leather black all over with red spots or hourglass shape on the underside of their spherical abdomen; males are brownish, much smaller, and have elongated abdomen with white and red markings on sides, lack red hourglass on abdomen

Length: 1.5"

Most spiders are not dangerous, but the black widow spider is one to be aware of. Widespread in Virginia, black widows are found in dark, moist, undisturbed places, such as wooded areas, rock walls, under buildings, and in woodpiles. Before indoor plumbing was common, it was always a good practice to check under the seat for spiders in outhouses before sitting down. Only the females bite if threatened; the much smaller males are harmless. Black widow spider bites cause redness, swelling, and severe muscle pain, but are very treatable, and rarely fatal in healthy adults. If bitten, wash the area with soap and water and stay calm but seek medical treatment right away. Black widows get their common name from the popular belief that the female sometimes eats the male after mating, but this rarely happens.

SIX-SPOTTED TIGER BEETLE
Cicindela sexguttata
Ground Beetle family (Carabidae)
Quick ID: metallic green with six white spots, large eyes, large white mandibles

Length: 0.47–0.55"

With over 2,600 species and as one of the most ferocious members of the insect class, tiger beetles are aggressive hunters with amazing predatory skills. Some tiger beetles can run over 5 miles per hour and relative to their size are among the fastest animals on earth. The six-spotted tiger beetles feed on insects, including ants, spiders, and caterpillars. They can often be seen running across hiking trails in the park.

Large milkweed bug

MILKWEED BEETLE
Tetraopes tetrophthalmus
Longhorned Beetle family (Cerambycidae)
Quick ID: bright orange-red with black spots, blackish legs, long blackish antennae

Length: 0.37–0.5"

The bright orange-red coloration of the milkweed beetle serves as a warning sign to predators. As the beetle feeds on milkweeds, it absorbs the toxic chemicals the plant produces. The toxins do not harm the beetle, but it becomes so distasteful that predators quickly learn not to try to feed on these brightly colored beetles. Adults emerge in June, and the larvae overwinter in the milkweed roots. Found abundantly worldwide, one out of every four animals is a beetle. Another orange insect you can see on milkweeds are the much flatter large milkweed bugs (*Oncopeltus fasciatus*) with its noticeable black back stripe, and small milkweed bugs (*Lygaeus kalmii*) with its reddish X.

Chestnut bark borer

LOCUST BORER BEETLE
Megacyllene robiniae
Longhorned Beetle family (Cerambycidae)
Quick ID: elongated body, dark brown with yellow markings, reddish-brown legs

Length: 0.47–0.78"

When the bright wands of goldenrod bloom in autumn, elongated beetles with colorful yellow markings often accompany them. The bright yellow-and-black warning colors mimic those of several wasp species. Locust borer beetles feed on the pollen of goldenrod but lay their eggs in black locust trees. The larvae hatch and hibernate under the bark. In spring the larvae tunnel into the tree, causing much damage. These pests of black locusts have spread across the United States, causing tree death in their wake. The similar chestnut bark borer (*Strophiona nitens*) may also be seen in spring.

DOGBANE BEETLE
Chrysochus auratus
Leaf Beetle family (Chrysomelidae)
Quick ID: oval, iridescent blue-green with a variety of metallic shades

Length: 0.31–0.43"

Less than 0.5 inch long, the stunningly beautiful dogbane beetle sparkles as it munches away on dogbane leaves. The iridescent greens, bronzes, blues, and coppers sparkle in the sunlight due to the structure of its wings, which have tiny, slanted plates that cover pigments underneath. The plates reflect light at various angles, which we see as different shades of color.

Adult lanternfly with nymphs

SPOTTED LANTERNFLY
Lycorma delicatula
Leaf Hopper family (Fulgoridae)
Quick ID: light brown front wings with black spots, brick-and-mortar pattern to end of front wings, red back wings with black spots and black and white bands; nymphs are black with white spots turning to red and black with white spots

Length: 1"

A new insect threat to Shenandoah arrived in Virginia in 2018. First discovered in neighboring Pennsylvania in 2014, the spotted lanternfly is native to Southeast Asia. These nonnative invasives pierce the bark to feed on the sap of over seventy species of plants, including grapevines, oaks, maples, walnuts, and fruit trees. This weakens the plant, leading to secondary infections and has caused destruction of grapevines and fruit trees. The spotted lanternfly is not known to bite, sting, or attack people. As the puffy grayish egg masses age, they darken and look like cracked mud. A key host tree of both nymphs and adults is the nonnative Tree-of-Heaven (*Ailanthus altissima*).

PERIODICAL CICADA
Magicicada septendecim
Cicada family (Cicadidae)
Quick ID: bulging red eyes, black body orange underneath, wings clear with orange veins

Length: 0.9–1.3"

Living underground into their teens, periodical cicadas have one of the most fascinating life cycles of all creatures. Sometimes called "seventeen-year-locusts," these insects surface every thirteen or seventeen years, shed their exoskeletons, and emerge as winged adults. Each brood has very specific emergence ranges and locations. To attract females, male cicadas vibrate two drum-like plates on each side of their abdomen 300 to 400 times per second, creating the characteristic hypnotic, buzzy drone heard in late summer. After mating, the females lay their eggs in end twigs of deciduous trees, causing the tips to turn brown and flag downward. The hatched nymphs drop to the ground,

Dog-day (swamp) cicada

burrow about a foot underground, and live off the sugars of tree roots. Virginia has twenty-five types of cicadas. Emerging in late July and August, the mottled green annual or "dog-day" cicadas (*Neotibicen sp.*), one of which is the swamp or morning cicada (*Neotibicen tibicen*), have black or greenish eyes. With a nutty flavor, protein-packed cicadas were traditionally cooked and eaten by American Indians. Adventurous chefs are rediscovering the foray into preparing meals using such insects.

HONEYBEE
Apis mellifera
Honey Bee family (Apidae)
Quick ID: reddish-brown with hairs, abdomen black with yellowish-orange bands

Length: 0.5–0.62"

Honeybees are not native to North America; they were introduced by early European settlers in the 1600s who used their honey as a sweetener in recipes, to heal wounds, and as an additive in soap to moisturize skin. The beeswax was used to make candles, to waterproof leather, and to bind wounds. Farmers built dome-topped woven straw beehives called "skeps" and kept hives of bees throughout the year.

HEMLOCK WOOLLY ADELGID
Adelges tsugae
Adelgid family (Adelgidae)
Quick ID: tiny, reddish-purple, aphid-like, covered by white waxy secretion

Length: 0.03"

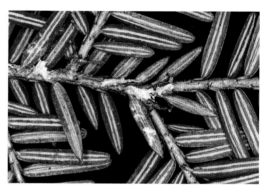

Introduced from East Asia, the hemlock woolly adelgid is a tiny aphid-like insect that, beginning in the mid-1980s, has decimated large stands of stately eastern hemlock trees. An adelgid is smaller than the period at the end of a sentence, but it damages hemlock trees by sucking sap from twigs. The needles dry out and fall off, followed by complete destruction of the branches. Trees often die within four years of infestation.

OAK TREEHOPPER
Platycotis vittata
Treehopper family (Membracidae)
Quick ID: grayish-green, triangular shaped, may have frontal horn, mottled with orange spots or red stripes

Length: 0.35–0.51"

Typically found on oak branches, oak treehoppers are a harmless and colorful addition to the forest. Over 3,000 species of treehoppers are found worldwide. Resembling thorns on a branch, some treehoppers have a horn-like extension on their head, while others have a helmet-shaped head. Treehoppers have beaks they use to pierce plant stems and feed on the sap but do little damage to the trees.

SEMISILKY ANT
Formica subsericea
Ant family (Formicidae)
Quick ID: blackish-brown abdomen with slightly silky sheen

Length: 0.12–0.25"

Allegheny ant mound

Ants are one of the most successful families of insects on earth. Roaming the planet for about 120 million years, only about half of the estimated more than 22,000 species of ants have been classified. The semisilky ant is the most abundant and widely distributed ant east of the Rocky Mountains. In a symbiotic relationship they tend leafhoppers and aphids in exchange for honeydew. Allegheny mound ants (*F. exsectoides*) construct huge conical mounds containing many galleries and chambers that may hold over one million ants. You can see these tall cone-shaped mounds in areas such as Gooney Manor Overlook at milepost 7.3 and near Old Rag Overlook at milepost 46.5.

DEER TICK
Ixodes scapularis
Hard Tick family (Ixodidae)
Quick ID: tiny, flat, black or dark brown; eight legs as adult, six legs as nymph; females have reddish abdomen

Length: 0.04–0.12"

Ticks are invertebrates placed in the Arachnid class along with spiders, mites, and scorpions. Four species of ticks found in Shenandoah are the deer tick, lone star tick (*Amblyomma americanum*), American dog tick (*Dermacentor variabilis*), and the brown dog tick (*Rhipicephalus sanguineus*). Ticks require a blood meal to pass through each of their three life stages—larva, nymph, and adult—and often wait on tall grass or the tips of leaves to catch a ride on a passing host. Deer ticks can transmit the bacterium that causes Lyme disease, the American dog tick and brown dog tick transmit the bacterium that causes Rocky Mountain spotted fever, and the lone star tick transmits the bacterium that causes human ehrlichiosis.

American dog tick male

Lone star tick female

American dog tick female

Lone star tick male

CHINESE PRAYING MANTIS
Tenodera sinensis
Mantid family (Mantidae)
Quick ID: tan to pale green, tan forewings with green along margin, compound eyes

Length: up to 5"

To other insects the praying mantis is seen as a giant green killing machine that lies in quiet wait before pouncing with lightning-fast arms on any prey that gets within its reach. Consuming nuisance insects such as mosquitoes and flies, the mantis will also eat other small invertebrates and even hummingbirds that get too close. The Chinese praying mantis was introduced from China in 1895 to help control pests. Another nonnative mantis, the European mantis (*Mantis religiosa*) grows to about 3 inches and can be distinguished by a round dark spot on the inner surface of its front legs. The native Carolina mantis (*Stagmomantis carolina*) is grayish green but only reaches about 2.5 inches long.

NORTHERN PYGMY CLUBTAIL
Lanthus parvulus
Clubtail family (Gomphidae)
Quick ID: black body with yellow markings, clear wings with a black dot on each wing

Length: 1.25"

Although uncommon throughout its range, the larvae of northern pygmy clubtail (or Zorro clubtail) loves Shenandoah's clear, cold streams. Dragonfly fossils date back about 325 million years. Dragonflies have long stout bodies and when perched extend their wings to each side. The related damselflies have long slender bodies and hold their wings above their bodies when perched. The long body and clasping "tail" of dragonflies causes some people to falsely believe they have stingers. Locally dragonflies are called "snake doctors," from the tale that they could stitch snakes back together if they were injured. They are also known as "devil's darning needles," referring to the supposed ability to sew naughty children's mouths closed.

COMMON TRUE KATYDID
Pterophylla camellifolia
Katydid family (Tettigoniidae)
Quick ID: leaf-green, oval wings with veins, rear wings shorter than front wings, upwardly pointed head

Length: 1.5–2.1"

The familiar song of the katydid ushers in the twilight with its lulling and repetitive "Katy-did Katy-didn't." From branches in the treetops, the males declare their territory, answering any rival's call. The species name *camellifolia* comes from the Greek word *camelo*, for the camel-like humped back, and the Latin word *folius*, which refers to the leaf-like appearance of the wings. Katydids produce their song by scraping a comb-like forewing across the edge of the opposing forewing.

NORTHERN WALKINGSTICK
Diapheromera femorata
Stick Insect family (Diapheromeridae)
Quick ID: brown to greenish brown, long thin body, long antennae

Length: 3–3.75"

Always a challenge to find, walking sticks have long, thin, cylindrical bodies with antennae about two-thirds the length of their 3-inch bodies. Their extremely camouflaged bodies resemble twigs on a branch, and often the only way to find one is to watch for a stick that moves in slow motion. Walkingsticks are a favorite prey item for certain birds, including American robins and crows. They can regenerate legs if they are lost in a foiled attack by a predator.

NORTH AMERICAN MILLIPEDE
Narceus americanus
Round-backed Millipede family (Spirobolidae)
Quick ID: purplish-brown body, thin red band on edge of each segment

Length: up to 4"

Entomologists (people who study insects and other arthropods) will tell you there are a lot of misconceptions about millipedes. Like ticks, spiders, centipedes, and pillbugs (sowbugs or roly-polys), millipedes are not insects, but arthropods. Insects have three body segments and six legs while millipedes have many segments. Millipedes have two legs on each side of most segments while centipedes have only one pair of legs on each segment. The common name "thousand-leggers" is a misnomer as most millipedes have only a few hundred legs. When disturbed, millipedes roll into a protective ball. Some millipedes secrete a fluid that smells like maraschino cherries or almonds and contains toxins to discourage predators from eating them.

FLOWERING DOGWOOD
Cornus florida
Dogwood family (Cornaceae)
Quick ID: rounded top, low spreading branches, greenish-yellow tiny flowers, white petal-like bracts, red fruit

Height: 10–35'

Flowering dogwood is one of the few trees that produces flowers before its leaves are fully unfurled. The four highly visible white bracts that resemble petals surround the inconspicuous, tiny greenish-yellow flowers. American Indians used the roots and bark medicinally for a variety of ailments, including headaches, diarrhea, worms, measles, and for making poultices for ulcers. A living emblem, the flowering dogwood shares the honor of being both the state flower and the state tree of Virginia. Unfortunately, this honored native tree is under attack by an introduced fungus, *Discula destructive*, which causes a deadly disease called *dogwood anthracnose* that kills the tree within a few years after it is infected.

BLACK GUM
Nyssa sylvatica
Dogwood family (Cornaceae)
Quick ID: alternate glossy leaves that
are oblong and 3–5 inches long, bark
with irregular ridges and diamond-
shaped plates, dark blue cherry-like
fruit

Height: 60–80'

One of the most noticeable trees in fall,
the leaves of black gum turn brilliant
scarlet red, adding cheery color to the
changing landscape. The bright leaves
are thought to attract resident and
migrating birds that enjoy the juicy dark blue fruits. The decayed branches of black gum provide denning
holes for raccoons and Virginia opossums. The genus name *Nyssa* refers to an ancient Greek mythological
water goddess or water nymph, and the species name *sylvatica* means "of the forest." This tree has many
common names, including tupelo, black tupelo, sour gum, and pepperidge.

REDBUD
Cercis canadensis
Pea family (Fabaceae)
Quick ID: heart-shaped leaves, purplish rose-colored pea-like flowers in tufts along the branches

Height: 20–30'

In spring the rosy-pink blooms of redbud are a signal that it is the beginning of a new year for nature. The short-lived flowers that bloom in early April to early May give way to flat 3-inch pods containing seeds that are eaten and scattered by birds and small mammals. American Indians and early settlers added the vitamin C–rich flowers to salads, and the tender young seedpods were eaten raw or cooked. The twigs were used to season meats such as venison and opossum and to produce a yellow dye. Most commonly found in the north section of the park, redbuds are especially stunning between the North Entrance and Dickey Ridge Visitor Center.

BLACK LOCUST
Robinia pseudoacacia
Pea family (Fabaceae)
Quick ID: white clustered flowers, short paired spines along twigs, alternate compound leaves with seven to nineteen oval leaflets

Height: 70–80'

Black locust is a fast-growing pioneer species that fills the spring air with its sweet fragrance from sweet-pea-like flowers that attract lots of pollinators. It is common in disturbed areas and open fields, but in a recovering forest is outcompeted by other trees such as oaks. Black locust wood is heavy, hard, and rot resistant, making it valuable for use as fence posts, rails, handles, flooring, and furniture. As firewood it produces little smoke and burns slowly. Dead black locust snags are important for use by cavity-nesting birds such as woodpeckers and owls. Bats may also roost in black locust cavities.

GRAY BIRCH
Betula populifolia
Birch family (Betulaceae)
Quick ID: grayish-white chalky bark, multiple trunks, double-toothed triangular leaves with long pointed tip, 2–3.5-inch male flowers hang down in catkins and 0.5-inch female flowers are erect

Height: 20–40'

Gray birch is a common tree in the northern states and Canada. In Virginia it is found only in the Big Meadows area and represents the southernmost native population of this special tree. Big Meadows is a unique high-elevation wetland habitat called a Northern Blue Ridge mafic fen and supports many state-rare species.

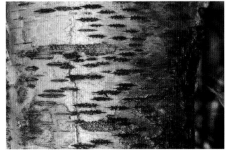

AMERICAN CHESTNUT
Castanea dentata
Beech family (Fagaceae)

Quick ID: traditionally tall and straight, new growth is only from shoots; flowers—long, creamy white, upright catkins; fruit—nuts in spiny seed pods; leaves—narrow, coarsely toothed, 4–8 inches long, 2–3 inches wide, tapering to a point

Height: 60–80'

The fall of the American chestnut from its reign as king of the Appalachian forests changed the course of many lives. Prior to the early 1900s, chestnut was one of the most important trees of the eastern forests. The broad boards were used for furniture, fences, homes, and barns—some of which can still be seen in park buildings. The nuts were roasted and eaten as treats as well as used to make breads, puddings, and soups. The leaves were used as a remedy for rheumatism, colds, and whooping cough. In 1904 an imported fungus, *Cryphonectria parasitica*, infected the trees and ended their lives. Short-lived shoots and small trees can still be seen in Shenandoah before they too succumb to the fungus.

WHITE OAK
Quercus alba
Beech family (Fagaceae)

Quick ID: spreading branches, rounded crown, dark green leaves with rounded lobes

Height: 60–100'

Widespread across eastern North America, the white oak is one of the key elements in deciduous woodland forests. This tall, majestic oak has wide, spreading branches and a rounded crown. The branches often spread horizontally, creating abundant shade underneath. The leaves have rounded lobes in contrast to the pointed lobes of red, black, and scarlet oaks. Early colonists used white oak lumber for shipbuilding and to make barrels for whiskey, wine, and other liquids. American Indians gathered the acorns in fall and soaked them in water several times to remove the tannins. After processing, the nuts were used for making bread, soups, and stews.

141

MOUNTAIN CHESTNUT OAK
Quercus montana
Beech family (Fagaceae)

Quick ID: alternate 5- to 9-inch-long oval leaves with rounded teeth, dark gray-brown bark deeply furrowed, acorn cap covers one-third of oval nut

Height: 60–80'

Chestnut oak has recently undergone a taxonomic name change from *Q. prinus* to *Q. montana* and is sometimes called rock chestnut oak or mountain chestnut oak. Unique among the thirteen species of oaks found in the park, the long oval leaves of chestnut oak have seven to sixteen pairs of rounded teeth that appear wavy and bear a resemblance to the shape of the leaves of American chestnut (*Castanea dentata*), which are sharply toothed. The dark gray-brown bark is the thickest of any eastern oak and forms deeply furrowed ridges. With the devastation of the American chestnuts in the early 1900s, former chestnut/oak forests are now dominated by chestnut oak, white oak (*Q. alba*), and northern red oak (*Q. rubra*).

MOCKERNUT HICKORY
Carya tomentosa
Walnut family (Juglandaceae)
Quick ID: alternate 9- to 14-inch-long compound leaves with seven to nine opposite toothed leaflets, leaf underside and twigs matted woolly with curly hairs, bark with diamond-shaped intersecting ridges, nuts round to egg-shaped with thick husk

Height: 50–80'

Five species of hickory trees can be found in Shenandoah, and they fill an important role in the forest ecosystem. The branches of hickories provide shelter for nesting birds, and many animals eat the large nuts. Several large species of moths use hickories as their larval food plants, including the luna moth and regal and walnut sphinx moths. Hickories have long leaves with smaller toothed leaflets. Mockernut hickory has seven to nine leaflets while most others have five to seven leaflets on each leaf. American Indians and early settlers prized the wood of hickory because it is hard, strong, and shock resistant. Hickory has been used for bows, tool handles, wheel spokes, baseball bats, and furniture as well as for curing meats.

RED OAK
Quercus rubra
Beech family (Fagaceae)
Quick ID: dull green hairless leaves with seven to nine lobes with bristle-like tips, dark bark furrowed with shiny striping

Height: 70–80'

Many woodland animals depend on the acorns of red oak, including black bears, white-tailed deer, and gray squirrels. The genus name for all oaks is *Quercus*. The species name *rubra* means "red." Oaks can be challenging to identify, but by comparing the details of leaves and acorns, you can usually differentiate the species. Red oak leaves are hairless underneath, and the non-hairy acorns' caps enclose only the base of the nut. Black oak (*Q. velutina*) has similar leaves, but they are slightly hairy beneath, and the acorns have a hairy cap. Found in the southern section of the park, scarlet oak (*Q. coccinea*) often has a bull's-eye pattern on the tip of the acorn, and the leaves are deeply lobed with rounded, thumb-shaped sinuses.

BLACK WALNUT
Juglans nigra
Walnut family (Juglandaceae)
Quick ID: 12- to 24-inch leaves with fifteen to twenty-three narrow leaflets, bark dark with diamond-shaped furrows, round green husk covering wrinkled brown nut

Height: 70–100'

Early colonists valued the walnut tree for its delicious nuts as well as its superior hardwood that was used in a variety of wood products. Extremely nutritional, walnuts contain a high level of antioxidants and are high in fiber. Walnuts were also used to make a brownish-black dye for graying hair and fabric and as a wood stain. The rich dark wood was prized for making furniture, cabinets, and gunstocks. The bark and nut rinds of the related butternut tree (*J. cinerea*), which is uncommon in the park, were used to dye the clothing of Confederate soldiers, earning them the nickname "butternut." Unlike smooth round walnuts, the nuts of butternut trees are hairy and oval.

SASSAFRAS
Sassafras albidum
Laurel family (Lauraceae)
Quick ID: small- to medium-size tree, leaves variable with two or three lobes or unlobed, dark blue berries with red stems

Height: 10–50'

Sassafras is a widespread small tree with leaves that resemble small mittens. The spicy-scented roots and bark were once used to make tea and to flavor root beer, but the active ingredient, safrole, is now known to cause cancer, and its use was banned in 1976. Spicebush swallowtail caterpillars rely on the leaves of sassafras and the related spicebush as a food source. In fall, birds enjoy the dark blue berries, and white-tailed deer browse the twigs. In 2002 the fungus *Raffaelea lauricola* was introduced into Georgia, carried by a beetle called the redbay ambrosia (*Xyleborus glabratus*). Infecting members of the laurel family, including sassafras and spicebush, the fungus causes a spreading deadly disease called laurel wilt.

EASTERN RED CEDAR
Juniperus virginiana
Cypress family (Cupressaceae)
Quick ID: evergreen leaves either scalelike or three-sided prickly needlelike; bark in shreds; hard, 0.25-inch, berry-like bluish-green cones

Height: 40–50'

American Indians and early settlers whose livelihood depended on knowing the natural resources that surrounded them valued the eastern red cedar, which is common throughout the eastern states. A pioneer species, it readily moves into cleared areas and the edges of fields and orchards. The durable aromatic wood from the eastern red cedar was heavily used for fence posts, clothes cabinets, and cedar chests. The heartwood was the source for pencils. The cones were used to flavor gin, and the fruits and leaves were used medicinally for colds and coughs. Many birds eat the berry-like cones, including the cedar waxwing. In the Shenandoah Valley, eastern red cedars are common in the area surrounding Cedar Creek and Belle Grove National Historic Park.

TULIP TREE
Liriodendron tulipfera
Magnolia family (Magnoliaceae)
Quick ID: tall straight trunk, tulip-shaped yellow-orange flowers, smooth leaves with four to six lobes

Height: 50–100'

On a fall afternoon in autumn, the tulip tree grove at milepost 8.0 becomes a showcase of magical light play as the yellow leaves reflect the long rays of the setting sun. Commonly known as tulip tree, tulip poplar, or yellow poplar, this tall straight tree is in the magnolia family but is called a poplar due to the wind-fluttered leaves that resemble the quaking leaves of poplars. The bowl-shaped yellowish-orange flowers look like large tulips and are pollinated by bees that in turn produce a dark, strong-tasting honey that was gathered by settlers for use in baking. Civil War doctors mixed the bark of tulip trees with willow bark as a remedy for fevers.

BALSAM FIR
Abies balsamea
Pine family (Pinaceae)

Quick ID: steeple-shaped evergreen, flat needles about 1 inch long and whitish beneath with broad circular base, purplish to green upright cones 1 to 3 inches long

Height: 40–60'

Most people are surprised to see a tree such as balsam fir in Shenandoah, as it is a tree of northern forests. Balsam fir reaches its southernmost limit in North America in Shenandoah National Park. It typically grows in the cool forests of Canada and the northeastern United States. American Indians used the sticky resin, called balsam, as a salve for burns, sores, and cuts. The sap was also chewed as a remedy for colds, and it was melted on stones and the fumes inhaled for headaches. During the Civil War the resin was used to treat battle wounds. It has also been used as a transparent glue for glasses and to prepare microscope slides.

RED SPRUCE
Picea rubens
Pine family (Pinaceae)
Quick ID: conifer, narrow conical crown, needles four-sided and curved with a sharp point, cones hang down

Height: 60–70'

More commonly found in cool New England states, red spruce grows in isolated populations in Virginia. It's found only in a few spots in Shenandoah but may once have been more common in these cool, moist mountains. This conifer is a valuable nesting site for birds, including yellow-rumped warblers. At present the spruce and fir at Big Meadows is this northern warbler's only known nesting spot in the southern Blue Ridge. Many of the high-altitude forests of massive red spruce trees were cut down by early settlers for timber and to make high-quality musical instruments such as guitars, violins, and pianos.

TABLE MOUNTAIN PINE
Pinus pungens
Pine family (Pinaceae)
Quick ID: evergreen, needles 1.5–3.5 inches long with usually two per bundle (sometimes three), cones stout and heavily armed with sharp, curved spines

Height: 40–60'

Table Mountain pine is endemic to the central and southern Appalachians. Perhaps the most outstanding and memorable character of this pine is its stout cones—handle these cones gingerly, as they are heavily armed with sharp, curved spines. The genus name *Pinus* refers to pines, and the species name *pungens* is from the Latin word *pungere*, which means "to pierce or sting." Table Mountain pine is typically found on dry, south- and southwest-facing slopes. It is dependent on fire to open its cones for dispersal of the seeds (a characteristic biologists call serotinous). In 1794 French botanist Andrew Michaux collected a specimen of this pine near Tablerock Mountain in Burke County, North Carolina—hence the common name.

VIRGINIA PINE
Pinus virginiana
Pine family (Pinaceae)
Quick ID: evergreen, whitish-green needles 1.5 to 3 inches long with two twisted needles per bundle; egg-shaped cones 1.5 to 2.75 inches with sharp, needle-like prickles; shaggy bark

Height: 30–40'

Virginia pine, or scrub pine, is an awkward, uncomely pine found in dry forests. A successional tree, it is one of the first trees to grow in disturbed areas. This hardy short pine has an irregular crown and prickly cones that remain on the tree for many years. Virginia pine is one of the four species of pines commonly seen in the park and is primarily a central and southern Appalachian endemic. Pitch pine (*P. rigida*) has three needles per bundle and tufts of needles fixed directly on the trunk. It has a high resin content; early colonists used pitch pine to make turpentine and tar for axle grease.

EASTERN HEMLOCK
Tsuga canadensis
Pine family (Pinaceae)
Quick ID: pyramidal evergreen, single flat 0.5-inch-long needles with two white lines below; 0.75-inch cone; drooping branches

Height: 60–70'

Handsome stands of centuries-old eastern hemlocks once graced the mountains of Shenandoah, and many bird species, including the Blackburnian warbler, nested in the tall branches. The bark was used as a source of tannin for the leather industry; the wood was used for railroad ties and to make paper. In an area of Shenandoah called the Limberlost, the hemlocks were reputedly saved by the owner of the Skyland Resort, George Freeman Pollock and his wife, Addie Nairn Pollock, who bought one hundred trees for $10 each. However, in the 1990s and early 2000s, a tiny nonnative insect called the hemlock woolly adelgid (*Adelges tsugae*) infested and destroyed most of these majestic trees, forever changing the face of Shenandoah.

DOWNY SERVICEBERRY
Amelanchier arborea
Rose family (Rosaceae)
Quick ID: small tree or shrub, showy star-shaped white flower, reddish-purple fruits

Height: 12–36'

Early in spring, before the redbud and dogwood begin to show their colors, the snow-white blossoms of downy serviceberry burst out like fresh white popcorn strewn about the forest. Serviceberry is a member of the rose family, which worldwide includes about 2,000 species of well-known plants and trees, including apples, plums, cherries, and mountain ash. The early settlers to the mountains knew spring was indeed on its way when the snow was melted and dirt roads cleared enough for the parson to venture into the small community churches for a Sunday service—hence the name serviceberry, or "sarvis" tree. The dark purplish fruits are still used to make jams, pies, wine, and are prized wildlife food. American Indians would crush serviceberries into a paste and allow it to dry. Dried berries were then mixed with dried meat and melted fat to be used in pemmican that could be stored in rawhide bags and the hardened mixture was eaten during the cold winter months.

APPLE
Malus pumila
Rose family (Rosaceae)
Quick ID: pinkish-white flowers with 5 rounded petals, finely toothed oval leaves, stout twisted trunk

Height: 20–30'

The Shenandoah Valley is famous for its large fields of sweet juicy apples that have been cultivated here for hundreds of years. In early May, residents celebrate the blooming of the apple trees with the annual Apple Blossom Festival in Winchester, Virginia. Many early settlers to the mountains cleared land and planted orchards in what was to eventually become Shenandoah National Park. One of the most recognized orchards was that of Thomas Milam, who lived in Madison County in the late 1780s. His 203-acre property was given as a land grant from Thomas Fairfax, Sixth Lord Fairfax of Cameron. In the park, look for apple trees in Milam Gap, Loft Mountain, Limberlost, Skyland, and other areas.

AMERICAN MOUNTAIN ASH
Sorbus americana
Rose family (Rosaceae)

Quick ID: alternate compound leaves, 11 to 17 pointed toothed leaflets, flat white flower clusters, bright red berries

Height: 15–30'

A small tree, American mountain ash is best recognized in the fall when the clusters of fire engine–red berries command attention. Although the berries are very tart, they sweeten after a frost and were traditionally used to make jellies and wines and were cooked with meat. Many birds, such as American robins, cedar waxwings, and juncos, gorge themselves on the ripe berries in fall. White-tailed deer browse on the leaves and twigs. Even though "ash" is in the common name and the leaves do resemble the shape of ash leaves, it is not related, and the leaves of ash trees are opposite rather than alternate. Look for American mountain ash in the Skyland area.

BLACK CHERRY
Prunus serotina
Rose family (Rosaceae)

Quick ID: white drooping flowers on stalk, shiny oblong finely toothed leaves, dark red fruit

Height: 60–80'

In spring, bees and other insects are attracted to the stalks of dangling, lacy white flowers of black cherry trees. The black cherry is a fast-growing pioneer species that can be found in many open, disturbed areas of Shenandoah. In fall numerous birds and mammals eat the deep red fruits, including black bears that climb into the branches to get to the juicy treats. Early settlers gathered the berries, which were eaten raw or made into jellies, jams, or desserts. The inner bark was made into tonics and used medicinally as cough syrup. The fine-grained wood of black cherry was highly prized by cabinet and furniture makers, who fashioned it into chairs, tables, and dressers.

STRIPED MAPLE
Acer pensylvanicum
Maple family (Aceraceae)

Quick ID: green bark with vertical white stripes, opposite double-toothed 5- to 8-inch leaves with 3 lobes and slightly yellowish and hairy beneath, light green flowers in long clusters, fruit in clusters of paired, wide-angled samaras (keys)

Height: 10–30'

An easy tree to identify, striped maple is a small understory tree named for the distinctive vertical white stripes on the green bark of young trees. Older trees have reddish-brown bark. The leaves are double-toothed with three lobes and resemble the foot of a goose. The big leaves were sometimes used as toilet paper. In May or June light green flowers hang in long clusters. The flowers are followed by fruits called samaras, or keys, that hang in pendulous chains in late summer. Known as "moosewood" in the northeast, it grows at high elevations in Shenandoah along with mountain maple (*A. spicatum*), which has smaller leaves with bigger teeth on the edges and lacks the white stripes on the bark.

Mountain maple

RED MAPLE
Acer rubrum
Maple family (Aceraceae)

Quick ID: opposite leaves with saw-toothed edges, 3 to 5 lobes, relatively shallow notches between lobes, whitish beneath; stems and twigs reddish; bark of older trees dark with thin flaky ridges; red clustered flowers; reddish paired forked keys (samaras)

Height: 60–90'

Even before winter has completely withdrawn its cold breath, the clusters of starry red flowers of red maple adorn its bare branches. Of the seven species of maples that can be found in Shenandoah, red maple is by far the most common and found throughout the park. American Indians boiled the inner bark as a wash for sore eyes. Although it does not produce as much sap as the sugar maple, they also used its sap to make maple syrup. The boiled inner bark was used to make blue, purple, and black dyes for fabrics. Red maple is most appreciated by visitors to the park for its bright scarlet autumn foliage.

TREE-OF-HEAVEN
Ailanthus altissima
Quassia family (Simaroubaceae)

Quick ID: alternate compound leaves 1 to 3 inches long with 11 to 41 leaflets, notch on base of leaflets

Height: 30–70'

Native to China, Tree-of-Heaven was brought to the United States in 1784 for use as a decorative garden plant and to add shade to city streets. It soon proliferated and spread rapidly across the country. A hardy fast-growing tree, it thrives in disturbed areas and spreads rapidly by suckers, often forming substantial colonies. Male flowers and crushed parts of the branches and leaves have an unpleasant strong odor, somewhat like that of rotten peanuts. Also known as ailanthus, it produces a chemical that inhibits the growth of other plants around it. Ailanthus is on the list of Virginia's most highly invasive plants along with garlic mustard (*Alliaria petiolata*), kudzu (*Pueraria montana*), mile-a-minute (*Polygonum perfoliatum*), and Japanese honeysuckle (*Lonicera japonica*).

153

PRINCESS TREE
Paulownia tomentosa
Paulownia family (Paulowniaceae)
Quick ID: paired 6- to 13-inch heart-shaped leaves that are hairy below; lavender trumpet-shaped clusters of flowers; winged seeds in dry, brown 4-sided capsules

Height: 30–60'

Princess tree was first introduced into the United States from Asia in the early 1800s for use as a fast-growing wood for export purposes. The tree did extremely well and spread throughout the east, outcompeting native trees in disturbed areas such as roadsides, stream banks, and forest edges. In spring the showy lavender flowers and the large heart-shaped leaves attract attention. Also known as "empress trees" or "royal paulownias," they are sometimes confused with catalpa trees, which have cigar-shaped seedpods. Now placed in their own family, Paulowniaceae, the name honors Anna Pavlovna (Paulowna) (1795–1865), daughter of Tsar Paul I of Russia.

HACKBERRY
Celtis occidentalis
Elm family (Ulmaceae)
Quick ID: alternate leaves with sharply toothed base; leaf rough on top but downy beneath; bark grayish, corky, and ridged with fine lines on surface; small dark purplish fruit

Height: 40–60'

Although the hackberry is not one of the most eye-catching trees in the forest, it is an important pioneer species of lower areas in the park and surrounding valleys. The graceful drooping branches have an awkward zigzag appearance, and the bark has corky projections. The leaves have a lopsided appearance, as they are unequal at the base. Hackberry is fast growing and tolerates wind and full sun. The dark fruits resemble small cherries and are favored by birds, including cedar waxwings and woodpeckers. The common name was apparently derived from *hagberry*, which means "marsh berry," a Scottish name for berry. The hackberry is the larval food plant for many butterflies, including the question mark, mourning cloak, hackberry, and American snout.

MOUNTAIN HOLLY
Ilex montana
Holly family (Aquifoliaceae)
Quick ID: multiple stems, deciduous alternate wrinkled 4-inch leaves that are whitish and hairy below, clusters of bright red berries

Height: 6–20'

Mountain holly, or winterberry holly, is a large shrub that is most noticeable in winter. Many hollies, such as the American holly (*I. opaca*) keep their evergreen leaves all year long, but the leaves of mountain holly turn yellow and drop off in the fall. In winter the bright red berries advertise their availability to potential takers to assist the plant in spreading its seeds away from the parent plant. Mountain holly is found throughout the park; look for it along the Limberlost Trail.

RED-PANICLED DOGWOOD
Cornus racemosa
Dogwood family (Cornaceae)
Quick ID: opposite oval leaves, small white flowers in long cone-shaped clusters, white fruits with red stems

Height: 6–12'

Along with flowering dogwood (*C. florida*), which grows to tree size, red-panicled dogwood is in the dogwood family but it only grows to shrub size. Also known as northern swamp dogwood, red-panicled dogwood has numerous stems that form thickets in moist areas. The bark is light gray, leading to the common name gray dogwood. The fruits, which are eaten by birds, are dull white, berry-like, one-seeded drupes in upright clusters called panicles that sit atop red stems. Red-panicled dogwood is conspicuous in Big Meadows in the winter.

CORALBERRY
Symphoricarpos orbiculatus
Honeysuckle family (Caprifoliaceae)
Quick ID: mounded shrub, opposite velvety oval leaves 1 to 1.5 inches long with soft hairs on lower surface, small greenish-white flowers, clusters of 0.25-inch coral-pink berries along arched stem

Height: 2–5'

The coral-colored berries of coralberry are most conspicuous in fall and winter. Coralberry spreads easily by rooting where it touches the ground, forming extensive impenetrable colonies in open areas and thickets that are used for shelter by small mammals such as cottontails. American robins eat the berries, and white-tailed deer browse on the leaves and twigs. American Indians used infusions of the leaves or bark as a wash for sore eyes. The wood was also made into charcoal and used in tattooing. In Virginia it is found primarily in the piedmont and mountains. Coralberry can be seen at Beahms Gap.

BLACK HUCKLEBERRY
Gaylussacia baccata
Heath family (Ericaceae)
Quick ID: 1- to 3-inch alternate egg-shaped leaves with yellowish dots on both sides, reddish flowers, bluish-black fruits

Height: 1–3'

In the long rays of the autumn sun, the reddened leaves of black huckleberry bushes cast a fiery glow across the rolling expanse of Big Meadows. Along with several other species of berry bushes, this prominent shrub plays an important role in the survival success of many wildlife species. Closely related to blueberries, huckleberries can be identified by the characteristic yellowish dots on the leaves called resin glands. The fruits of blueberries also contain more tiny seeds than those of huckleberries. In spring, does hide their fawns under the protective dense foliage of huckleberries while they graze at a distance, always keeping a watchful eye on their young.

MOUNTAIN LAUREL
Kalmia latifolia
Heath family (Ericaceae)
Quick ID: 2- to 5-inch leathery pointed evergreen leaves, bowl-shaped pink flowers

Height: 6–10'

In May and June, Shenandoah bursts with pink blossoms as the blooms of mountain laurel revel in the warm breezes. The anthers of the pastel-pink, saucer-shaped flowers are held in a curved backward arch by two small clasps. When a bee visits the flower, it triggers the release of the anther, which catapults pollen onto the back of the bee for it to carry to the next flower, aiding in pollination. The shrubs form thickets of impenetrable gnarly branches, which are locally known as "laurel hells" or "ivy thickets." Mountain laurel tends to grow best on southern-facing slopes, ridges, and hillsides. The Appalachian Trail passes through lovely stands of mountain laurel at Jenkins Gap and Sawmill Ridge.

MALEBERRY
Lyonia ligustrina
Heath family (Ericaceae)

Quick ID: leaves alternate, oblong, finely toothed (serrated) with pointed tip, lighter green below with hairs; clusters of white urn-shaped flowers; fruit a 0.25-inch dry brown 5-parted capsule

Height: 3–6'

Along with huckleberries and blueberries, maleberry is a member of the heath family. The genus name *Lyonia* honors John Lyon, a Scottish botanist who explored the southern Appalachians in the early 1800s. Found in the broad expanse of Big Meadows, maleberry is a dense shrub that plays an important role in shelter and offers cover for wildlife. In spring the clusters of white, broad-based, urn-shaped flowers attract small insects and bees. Present most of the year, a good way to identify this shrub are the light brown, dry seed capsules that open into five sections. Maleberry does not produce the fleshy fruits of blueberries and huckleberries.

GREAT RHODODENDRON
Rhododendron maximum
Heath family (Ericaceae)
Quick ID: 3- to 14-inch large leathery oblong leaves with rolled edges, white flowers with pinkish tinge and usually some green dots

Height: 10–30'

Growing in shaded woods, great rhododendrons are large evergreen shrubs with big oblong leaves that remain on the branches for several years before dropping off. The clusters of white blossoms are tinged with pink and are spotted inside with green markings. Bees, butterflies, and hummingbirds pollinate the flowers. Although great rhododendrons are uncommon in Shenandoah, they are one of the shrubs characteristic of the southern Appalachians. Known locally as laurel, great laurel, or rosebay rhododendron, they are common along the Blue Ridge Parkway, which joins Shenandoah with Great Smoky Mountains National Park. Great rhododendrons bloom in late June and can be seen near Camp Rapidan along the Laurel Prong Trail.

PINXTER AZALEA
Rhododendron periclymenoides
Heath family (Ericaceae)
Quick ID: 2- to 4-inch oval leaves, clusters of pale pink tubular flowers with long protruding stamens

Height: 6–12'

Pinxter azalea, or pinxter flower, blooms early in Shenandoah. The characteristic five long, protruding stamens and one pistil in the large, pink, funnel-shaped flowers are an easy way to identify this tall deciduous shrub, sometimes called pink azalea. Its pink flowers appear in May often before the leaves have fully unfurled. The common name pinxter comes from the Dutch word for Pentecost, as this flower blooms about a month and a half after Easter. Look for it scattered along Skyline Drive.

MINNIEBUSH
Rhododendron pilosum
Heath family (Ericaceae)
Quick ID: oval 1- to 2-inch hairy leaves with glands along midrib of leaf below with whitish tips, bell-shaped white to yellowish-pink flowers, fruit is a dry capsule with 4 sections

Height: 1–6'

A low-growing southern and central Appalachian endemic, minniebush has bell-shaped, yellowish-pinkish flowers that resemble blueberry flowers, but the leaves resemble azaleas. In 2011 the genus was changed from *Menziesia* to *Rhododendron* when DNA evidence revealed that it is more closely related to rhododendrons than previously thought. Common in the south section of the park, minniebush grows with other members of the heath family in acidic soils, often on rocky areas. It blooms May through July.

ROSESHELL AZALEA
Rhododendron prinophyllum
Heath family (Ericaceae)
Quick ID: alternate 1- to 3-inch-long oblong leaves that are woolly beneath, woolly twigs and buds, rosy-pink tubular flowers with relatively long stamens

Height: 6–10'

Scattered throughout the park, roseshell azalea is a native shrub that puts on a great show during May and June. Shenandoah is one of the best places to see the lovely rose-pink flowers that produce a spicy-sweet cinnamon clove fragrance. South of Shenandoah, along the North Carolina section of the Blue Ridge Parkway, this species is found in only one isolated spot. Roseshell azalea has a number of common names, including rose azalea and early azalea. Taxonomically the species name has been changed from *R. roseum* to *R. prinophyllum*. The flowers open as the leaves are first appearing and are pollinated by ruby-throated hummingbirds and butterflies such as swallowtails.

BLUE RIDGE BLUEBERRY
Vaccinium pallidum
Heath family (Ericaceae)
Quick ID: small shrub that forms colonies; alternate hairless leaves that are 1.25 to 2 inches; elliptical, finely toothed and 0.6 to 1 inch broad; bell-shaped pink to greenish-white flowers; blue berries

Height: 9–20"

Common in the park in dry woods and thickets, Blue Ridge blueberry is also known as southern low blueberry, upland low blueberry, or hillside blueberry. Blue Ridge blueberry is very similar in appearance to late low blueberry (*V. angustifolium*), both of which can be found in Shenandoah. The leaves of late low blueberry are sometimes hairy or whitened below, and the twigs are also sometimes hairy. In contrast the twigs of Blue Ridge blueberry are never hairy, and the leaves are never hairy or whitened below. The leaves of Blue Ridge blueberry are also a bit longer and broader than those of late low blueberry. Many species of mammals and birds eat the berries. In fall the leaves turn crimson red in Big Meadows.

DEERBERRY
Vaccinium stamineum
Heath family (Ericaceae)
Quick ID: alternate oval leaves with pointed ends and whitish underneath, white flowers with broad bell shape and long yellow stamens, greenish-blue berries with dusty white coating (bloom)

Height: 1.6–4.9'

Deerberry is a common shrub of meadows and forest edges where deer forage on the leaves and twigs. The berries are bitter but readily eaten by birds and deer, and the seeds are spread through their waste products. Deerberry can survive and even benefit from fires because the plant can spread by underground root-like structures called rhizomes. The white flowers that bloom in May and June are a flared bell shape, and the yellow stamens project from the end like tiny bell clappers.

WITCH HAZEL
Hamamelis virginiana
Witch-hazel family (Hamamelidaceae)
Quick ID: wavy-toothed oval leaves, crumply yellow flowers in late fall, fruit a hard woody capsule

Height: 10–25'

BEAKED HAZELNUT
Corylus cornuta
Birch family (Betulaceae)
Quick ID: loose multiple stems, oval leaves coarsely double-toothed and hairy underneath, smooth gray bark, flowers in catkins, fruit a nut enclosed in a husk with tubular "neck"

Height: 2–10'

The unusual elongated husks covering the nut of the beaked hazelnut somewhat resemble the beak of a bird—hence the common name. The nuts of the closely related American hazelnut (*C. americana*) lack the "beak" and instead are enclosed in thin, flattened, round husks with fringes on the end. The nuts, called filberts, are edible and were collected and stored by American Indians to help them survive the long winters. The genus name *Corylus* is Latin for "hazel," and the species name *cornuta* is from the Latin for "horn or antler" in reference to the shape of the fruit.

After the colorful leaves of autumn have blazed their way into brown crinkles, the yellow flowers of witch hazel burst into bloom. The common name witch comes from an old English word that means "bendable." Like the hazel trees in Europe, the forked branches of witch hazel were traditionally used as divining rods. A forked branch was broken off, and the Y was held in both hands with the stem of the Y pointed toward the ground. When the stick started vibrating, it supposedly meant that water was near. Witch hazel has long been used as an astringent to improve skin tone.

SPICEBUSH
Lindera benzoin
Laurel family (Lauraceae)
Quick ID: alternate simple 4-inch leaves, small yellow flowers in clusters, red berry-like fruit

Height: 6–12'

Spicebush is a native shrub in the eastern states and is one of the first plants to bloom in spring. When rubbed the leaves and twigs of this shrub produce a spicy, aromatic scent. The crushed aromatic leaves were used by early settlers as an invigorating spicy-smelling aftershave. The stems and leaves were added to roasts of wild game, such as opossum or groundhog, and were also used to brew tea. Spicebush swallowtail butterflies lay their eggs on the leaves of spicebush. The newly emerged caterpillars look like black-and-white bird droppings, but later are smooth green with eyespots that resemble a snake's head. When they are not feeding, they fold the leaves over them like a tent for shelter.

WILD HYDRANGEA
Hydrangea arborescens
Hydrangea family (Hydrangeaceae)
Quick ID: many unbranched stems, opposite heart-shaped leaves 4 to 10 inches long with toothed margin, white flowers in flat-topped clusters 2 to 6 inches across, fruit a dry capsule, orange-brown shredding bark

Height: 3–6'

Most people are familiar with hydrangeas as popular ornamental shrubs grown for their large pompom-like flowers the color of which is affected by the soil's pH. Wild hydrangea is a native shrub with flat-topped, umbrella-shaped clusters of white flowers that bloom in June and July. It is sometimes called smooth hydrangea for its smooth twigs or sevenbark for the bark's tendency to shed into successive layers with different colors. Northern bush honeysuckle (*Diervilla lonicera*) has similar leaves, but the flowers are yellow and the twigs have slender ridges. Wild hydrangea was used medicinally by American Indians for burns, tumors, high blood pressure, sore muscles, and gall bladder troubles.

Northern bush honeysuckle

ALLEGHENY BLACKBERRY
Rubus alleghaniensis
Rose family (Rosaceae)
Quick ID: arching angular stems with stout prickles, alternate fan-shaped leaves with 3 to 7 serrated leaflets that are pale below, gland-tipped hairs on branches, flowers with 5 white petals, juicy black berries

Height: 3–6'

To children who grew up in the mountains, blackberry picking was an enjoyable chore. The only thing that tasted better than freshly picked blackberries were perhaps the pies, muffins, and jams to come. Unfortunately, to get to the berries one had to suffer through the needle-sharp prickles that seem to reach out and grab fingers and shirtsleeves. The long arching stems of Allegheny blackberry form dense thickets, providing perfect shelter for many species of wildlife, including rabbits and skunks. Blackberry roots, leaves, or stems were used as a traditional home remedy for diarrhea. Twelve species of blackberries, raspberries, and similar berries (including Allegheny blackberry) are found in Shenandoah.

PURPLE-FLOWERING RASPBERRY
Rubus odoratus
Rose family (Rosaceae)

Quick ID: large maple-like leaves, thornless, bristly hairs on stems, rose-purple flower with 5 petals, red flattened berries

Height: 3–6'

Lining much of Skyland Drive, the rambling stems of purple-flowering raspberry, or flowering raspberry, form large patches in disturbed areas, roadsides, and open hillsides. The large maple-like leaves flap lazily in the breezes, revealing their whitish underside. In early summer the rose-purple flowers attract bees and other insects. The flattened, bland berries have fuzzy hairs but were used by early mountain settlers to make jelly. American Indians used the roots medicinally as a remedy for a variety of ailments, including coughs, toothaches, boils, and diarrhea.

WHITE MEADOWSWEET
Spiraea alba var. latifolia
Rose family (Rosaceae)

Quick ID: numerous erect unbranched stems, alternate narrow elliptical 2- to 3-inch finely toothed leaves, clusters of starry white flowers, fruit a dry capsule

Height: 3–6'

In midsummer the starry white flowers of white meadowsweet can be found in moist meadows such as Big Meadows in Shenandoah. Also known as narrowleaf spirea, northern meadowsweet, or simply meadowsweet, this plant produces white flowers arranged in pyramid-shaped spikes.

SMOOTH SUMAC
Rhus glabra
Sumac family (Anacardiaceae)

Quick ID: shrubby and multistemmed; alternate leaves 12 to 18 inches long with 11 to 31 lance-shaped leaflets per leaf, each 2 to 4 inches long with toothed edges, pale green and hairy below; upright clusters of small hairy fruits (drupes); stems lack hairs

Height: 10–15'

One relative of the sumac family, poison sumac (*Toxicodendron vernix*) has led to the common misconception that all sumacs are poisonous. In fact, poison sumac only grows in boggy areas and is not found in Shenandoah at all. Sumacs

grow quickly in colonies and can be seen at many overlooks in the park, where their fall colors of reds and oranges brighten the view. American Indians used the red fruits as a lemonade-like drink. The fruits were also used as a remedy for diarrhea and bedwetting, and to ease painful menstrual cramps. The stems of staghorn sumac (*R. typhina*) are covered in hairs. Thin leafy "wings" border the leaf midrib of winged sumac (*R. copallinum*).

COMMON ELDERBERRY
Sambucus canadensis
Viburnum family (Viburnaceae)

Quick ID: opposite compound 6- to 11-inch leaves, 5 to 7 toothed leaflets, creamy white flowers in broad dense flat-topped clusters, blackish-blue fruits

Height: 3-13'

Scattered through the park, common elderberry is found in fields, roadsides, and other disturbed areas. In spring, the large plate-sized clusters of creamy white flowers of this lanky shrub fade into fronds of juicy blue-black berries. The plant contains a chemical similar to cyanide and can be toxic to humans. Eating the uncooked or unripe green berries can cause diarrhea or vomiting. Cooking the berries makes them safe to eat and they are prized for use in pies, jellies, pancakes, syrups, and wine. Long used medicinally, parts of the plant have been used as a remedy for colds, flu, fevers, constipation, and skin conditions. Elderberries are high in vitamins A and C, and they contain more cancer-fighting antioxidants than blueberries or cranberries. Some recent studies suggest the antiviral properties of elderberry extract significantly reduce the symptoms of influenza.

RED ELDERBERRY
Sambucus racemosa
Moschatel family (Adoxaceae)
Quick ID: opposite compound leaves with 5 to 7 serrated leaflets, dome-shaped clusters of tiny white flowers, dome-shaped clusters of red berries

Height: 8–20'

Found at mid- to high elevations in the park, red elderberry, or red-berried elder, has compound leaves with five to seven lance-shaped, finely toothed leaflets. Common elderberry (*S. canadensis*) typically grows in more open areas, especially in the valleys surrounding the park, and has blue-black berries rather than the bright red berries of red elderberry. The berries of both species are toxic, but cooking makes them safe to eat. Look for red elderberry in the Marys Rock area and at Hemlock Springs Overlook.

BLACKHAW
Viburnum prunifolium
Moschatel family (Adoxaceae)
Quick ID: opposite elliptical finely toothed leaves, small white flowers in flat clusters, blue-black berries

Height: 12–15'

Home gardeners are familiar with viburnums as medium to large perennial shrubs that add subtle but interesting dimension to landscape design. Some introduced viburnums may be found around old homesteads, including the "snowball" viburnums (*V. opulus* and *V. plicatum*). In the wild, native viburnums act as important shelter for small mammals and birds and provide nourishing fruit for wildlife in the winter. The fruits of blackhaw resemble the fruits of hawthorn trees—hence the common name "haw." The ripening fruits become wrinkled, resembling raisins, and are eaten by birds. Blackhaw was used medicinally as an aid for menstrual cramps and to prevent miscarriages, but it is now known that it may cause mutations in unborn babies.

ORIENTAL BITTERSWEET
Celastrus orbiculatus
Bittersweet family (Celastraceae)
Quick ID: twining woody stem 30 feet or longer, orange berries with yellow pods, alternate round leaves

One of the most invasive plants in North America, oriental bittersweet has bright reddish-orange fruits along a long twining vine. Introduced into the US in the 1860s, oriental bittersweet is an aggressive climbing vine that competes with and often displaces the native American bittersweet (*C. scandens*). Gathered for fall decorations and flower arrangements, American bittersweet populations are now in decline and this practice is discouraged.

American Indians used a compound of the bittersweet root to ease the pain of childbirth and for coughs. Birds are attracted to the cheery bright fruits in fall, but human ingestion can cause vomiting and diarrhea.

Roundleaf greenbrier fruits

Carrion flower

ROUNDLEAF GREENBRIER
Smilax rotundifolia
Catbrier family (Smilacaceae)

Quick ID: clusters of small greenish-yellow flowers, alternate round to heart-shaped leaves, dark blue-black berries in clusters, stiff prickles

A common vine of woodlands, greenbrier is often unnoticed by hikers unless you happen to brush into the sharp prickles. They are commonly called catbriers due to the cat claw–like prickles. Roundleaf greenbrier is a native, 10- to 20-foot vine that uses thin tendrils to climb up trees and over shrubs. The twining vines provide shelter for small

Carrion flower fruits

mammals and birds. The dark bluish-black berries often stay on the vine into winter, and numerous birds eat them, including northern cardinals, mockingbirds, and sparrows. American Indians ate the roots for food and used the leaves as a rub for rheumatism, scalds, and cuts. The foul-smelling flowers of the related carrion flower (*S. herbaceae*) attract carrion flies as their pollinators.

VIRGINIA CREEPER
Parthenocissus quinquefolia
Grape family (Vitaceae)
Quick ID: 5 palmate toothed leaflets 4 to 8 inches
across, bluish-black berries, small greenish flowers

Climbing over trees and rocky slopes throughout
the park, Virginia creeper is most noticeable in
fall when the leaves turn brilliant red offset by the
bluish-black berries. Although toxic to humans,
the berries of Virginia creeper are an important
food source for squirrels and many birds, including
American robins, woodpeckers, thrushes, gray
catbirds, mockingbirds, and chickadees. Virginia
creeper is sometimes mistaken for poison ivy, but it
has five leaves rather than the characteristic three leaves of poison ivy.

SUMMER GRAPE
Vitis aestivalis
Grape family (Vitaceae)
Quick ID: alternate toothed heart-shaped leaves, small greenish flowers, dark blue berries with a whitish
dusting hanging in clusters

Grapes are widely used as a food source for wildlife, including black bears, white-tailed deer, Virginia
opossums, raccoons, and numerous birds. Early settlers gathered wild grapes to use in jellies, juices, and
wines. At his plantation in Monticello, Thomas Jefferson failed in his attempt to start vineyards, as the
European grape varieties he planted did not survive in Virginia. Summer grapes are native to North America
and possess excellent resistance to diseases that affect nonnative species of grapes. In 1826 a Virginia
physician, Daniel Norton, succeeded in hybridizing a European grape with summer grape to make a winning
cultivar called the "Norton" grape, which is still used successfully in the Virginia wine industry.

PURPLE CLEMATIS
Clematis occidentalis
Buttercup family (Ranunculaceae)
Quick ID: leaves with 3 oval leaflets, flowers with 4 bluish-purple urn-shaped sepals

Blooming in May and June, purple clematis, or mountain clematis, gracefully drapes over the limbs of shrubs and small trees. The lilac-colored flowers have four modified sepals that look like petals. In some species the sepals are tough and leathery—hence the common name "leatherflowers." Fused at the base, the sepals curl back at the tips, forming a graceful urn-shaped flower. The flowers are followed by tufts of silvery, feathery fruits called achenes. Achenes are dry, one-seeded fruits with the outer wall enclosing the seed. In clematis vines the achene has a long, fuzzy-spiraled tail. In autumn the clusters of feathery achenes create a dramatic show, covering rocky hillsides in the park. Shenandoah is one of the best places to see purple clematis, which is uncommon elsewhere in Virginia. Look for this vine on Miller's Head Trail.

VIRGIN'S BOWER
Clematis virginiana
Buttercup family (Ranunculaceae)
Quick ID: leaves opposite with 3 sharply toothed leaflets, 4-petaled creamy-white 1-inch starry flowers

In summer the graceful vines of virgin's bower climb over shrubs, fences, and rocky areas producing clusters of starry, creamy-white flowers that attract butterflies and hummingbirds. It is sometimes called "old man's beard" or the "devil's darning needles" because of the grayish plumes of feathery seeds resembling large powder puffs that grace the roadsides in fall. Although virgin's bower can cause skin irritation if touched, it was used by American Indians for stomach and kidney problems. The roots were powdered and used on sores caused by venereal disease. American Indians also used the leaves of virgin's bower as a cleansing emetic ingredient in the curative rite called the Green Corn Ceremony, when the new crop of corn was celebrated.

POISON IVY
Toxicodendron radicans
Sumac family (Anacardiaceae)
Quick ID: 3 leaflets with pointed tips each 2 to 4.5 inches long, climbing vine or trailing vine or shrub

Poison ivy contains urushiol, which is an oil that causes a skin reaction in 80 percent of people, and although most people have heard the saying "leaves of three, let it be," there are quite a few plants that resemble poison ivy. One of the most common vines mistaken for poison ivy is Virginia creeper, which has not three but five leaves. Poison sumac is not found in the park. Poison ivy can be a trailing vine from 4 to 10 inches tall, or it can grow up to 150 feet into trees with a vine that looks like a thick fuzzy rope. Birds eat the greenish-white fruit.

Poison ivy rootlets

HAZEL DODDER
Cuscuta coryli
Morning Glory family (Convolvulaceae)
Quick ID: thin whitish to yellowish-orange vine
encircling other plants, tiny bell-shaped white
flowers, scalelike leaves

Often covering wayside shrubs and vegetation
like a batch of last night's spaghetti, the long,
thin, yellowish-orange vines of dodder sometimes
blanket other plants in large net-like masses.
A curiosity of the plant world, dodder reacts
to airborne chemicals given off by various
plants—essentially smelling the plants. Rejecting
inappropriate plants, it responds to the chemicals
by sending out long tendrils toward a suitable
plant. As it does not produce its own chlorophyll,
dodder is totally dependent on other plants for
its nourishment. It presses little bumps called
haustoria into the host plant, which allow it to
leach out nutrients that it needs to survive. Five
species of dodders have been found in Shenandoah.

COW PARSNIP

Heracleum maximum
Carrot family (Apiaceae)
Quick ID: large 4- to 8-inch flat clusters of
small white flowers, maple-like leaves up to 12
inches, very tall grooved hairy stem

Height: 3–10' Bloom Season: June–August

Towering above Skyline Drive, the white, dinner
plate–size flowers of cow parsnip sway in the
summer breezes. The genus name *Heracleum*
refers to the mythologic Hercules, and the
species name *maximum* refers to the plant's
great size, which may reach up to 10 feet tall. American Indians ate the young stems of cow parsnip like
cooked celery and used the plant medicinally for rashes, blisters, warts, and rheumatism. The roots were
used to make a yellow dye; they have also been shown to have antifungal and anti-mycobacterial properties
and are being tested for antiviral properties.

JACK-IN-THE-PULPIT
Arisaema triphyllum
Arum family (Araceae)

Quick ID: 3 oval leaflets atop a stem, spike of tiny greenish-yellow flowers covered by light green hood with white or purplish stripes, red berries in clusters

Height: 8–24" Bloom Season: April–June

The unusual shape of this wildflower has given imaginative botanists the opportunity to personify it as a parson in his arching pulpit. The parson (Jack) is

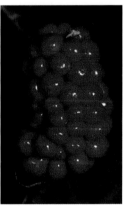

a spike called a spadix, which is covered in tiny greenish-yellow flowers. Gnats, fungus flies, and other tiny insects pollinate the flowers. The arching pulpit covering the parson is a leafy structure called a spathe. The leaves and thick root-like structure called a corm contain crystals of calcium oxalate, which cause intense burning if eaten, therefore providing protection from grazing wildlife. American Indians dried the corms for six months then used them as a liniment, on boils, and for throat irritations.

WHITE SNAKEROOT
Ageratina altissima
Aster family (Asteraceae)
Quick ID: opposite oval to heart-shaped leaves with serrated margins, flat heads of 12 to 25 white flowers

Height: 1–4' Bloom Season: July–October

One of the last flowers to bloom in summer, white snakeroot's roots were used by early settlers to treat snakebites. Not a favored wildlife plant, it is bitter and contains a toxin called tremetol. Unfortunately, cows are indiscriminate grazers, and when cattle consume white snakeroot, the toxin contaminates the milk. In the 1800s many people—including Abraham Lincoln's mother—were killed by a mysterious malady that no one could identify. The mystery was finally solved by a physician, Dr. Anna Pierce Hobbs Bixby, who methodically studied the disease and traced the deaths to consumption of tainted milk and butter. During her research she befriended a Shawnee woman, who may have played a key role in the discovery of "milk sickness."

SWEET SCENTED JOE-PYE WEED
Eutrochium purpureum
Aster family (Asteraceae)
Quick ID: flat-topped clusters of pinkish-purple flowers, narrow lance-shaped leaves whorled around the tall stem

Height: 2–6' Bloom Season: July–October

Joe-pye weed and its relatives, including boneset (*Eupatorium perfoliatum*) have long been used for medicinal purposes. This plant is sometimes called "gravel root," as it was traditionally used to treat "gravel" or kidney stones. American Indians used the roots of the plant as a treatment for rheumatism, gout, swelling, or "dropsy," and for kidney and urinary tract problems. Joe-pye weeds attract numerous insects and butterflies for pollination. Sweet-scented Joe-pye weed has recently undergone a change in genus from *Eupatorium* to *Eutrochium* to better reflect the original genus.

WOODLAND SUNFLOWER
Helianthus divaricatus
Aster family (Asteraceae)
Quick ID: 10 or more ray flowers and yellow disk flowers, leafy stems, (usually) stemless opposite leaves

Height: 2–6' Bloom Season: June–August

The original sun worshippers, sunflowers stretch their showy yellow flower heads toward the sun during the hot summer months. The genus name *Helianthus* comes from the Greek word *helios*, which means "sun," and *anthos*, which means "flower." Members of the aster family, woodland sunflowers can be distinguished from other sunflowers by the opposite leaves that are usually stemless. Many birds eat the seeds of these wildflowers, including American goldfinches and tufted titmice. These and other sunflowers often form dense colonies that provide shelter for small mammals, such as cottontail rabbits. White-tailed deer sometimes browse on the leaves and stems.

GOLDEN RAGWORT
Packera aurea
Aster family (Asteraceae)
Quick ID: golden-yellow daisy-like flowers, heart-shaped basal leaves that are purple underneath, alternate lance-shaped divided stem leaves

Height: 12–30" Bloom Season: April–August

Also known as golden groundsel or squaw weed, golden ragwort adds a relaxed decor of cheerful yellow flowers to park roadsides and meadows. The disorganized arrangement of ten to twelve ray flowers surrounds the inner sphere of deep yellow disc flowers that contain the reproductive parts. The roots and leaves were traditionally used to treat menstrual and heart problems, but scientists have discovered that this plant contains alkaloids that are highly toxic and can cause liver damage. The genus name *Packera* honors John G. Packer, a Canadian botanist, and the species name *aurea* is Latin for "golden." This flower was formerly classified as *Senecio aureus*.

BLACK-EYED SUSAN
Rudbeckia hirta
Aster family (Asteraceae)
Quick ID: bright yellow ray flowers with dark blackish-brown center, alternate lance-shaped to oval bristly hairy leaves, bristly hairy stem

Height: 1–3' Bloom Season: June–October

Perhaps no other wildflower is as easily recognized as the familiar daisy-like, bright yellow flowers of black-eyed Susans. The genus name *Rudbeckia* honors a Swedish botanist, Olaus Rudbeck; *hirta* is in reference to the hairs on the leaves and stems, which act as a deterrent for insects such as ants. The yellow outer petals are called ray flowers and attract pollinators such as butterflies. The black "eye" is composed of disk flowers that eventually become the seeds enjoyed by many species of birds.

WRINKLE-LEAF GOLDENROD
Solidago rugosa
Aster family (Asteraceae)
Quick ID: large pyramid-shaped flower head with numerous golden-yellow flowers on top of stems, alternate rough-toothed leaves, hairy rough stem

Height: 1–5' Bloom Season: July–September

Like many members of the aster family, the seventeen species of goldenrods found in the park provide an identification challenge for wildflower lovers. Wrinkle-leaf, or rough-stemmed, goldenrod has a characteristic rough hairy stem and wrinkled leaves due to deep venation. Goldenrods attract a variety of insects. Look closely and you may be able to spot an ambush bug or a goldenrod spider sitting quietly on the flower. Both are well camouflaged to the colors of the goldenrod and wait in stillness for a prey insect to happen by. Some people mistakenly think goldenrods cause airborne allergies, but the thick, heavy pollen sticks on insects and does not float on the air.

WAVYLEAF ASTER
Symphyotrichum undulatum
Aster family (Asteraceae)
Quick ID: light purple flowers with yellow center about 0.75 inch across, rough wavy-margined leaves with winged stems that clasp the plant's hairy stem

Height: 1–3' Bloom Season: August–October

Wavyleaf aster is commonly seen along Skyline Drive when the trees are displaying their fall colors. Also known as the composite family, the aster family is a huge family with 1,500 to 1,700 genera containing 20,000 to 25,000 species of plants ranging from herbaceous plants and vines to trees. Asters have ray flowers that are often bright purple, pink, or white to attract insects. They also have central disc flowers that contain the nectar and reproductive parts. Common in woodlands, dry forests, and road banks, wavyleaf aster has recently undergone a name change from *Aster undulatus* to *Symphyotrichum undulatum*.

COMMON MILKWEED
Asclepias syriaca
Dogbane family (Apocynaceae)
Quick ID: pinkish flowers in round clusters, oval opposite leaves hairy underneath

Height: 3–5' Bloom Season: June–August

The upright pink flowers of common milkweed are among the nine species of milkweeds that bloom in Shenandoah, including the pale nodding flowers of poke milkweed (*A. exaltata*) and the pinkish starry heads of four-leaved milkweed (*A. quadrifolia*). Many insects thrive on milkweed, including the milkweed beetle, which is red with black spots, and the orange and black large milkweed bugs. Monarch caterpillars feed on the leaves of milkweeds. In the fall the seeds are blown from the plant and carried about on silken parachutes. During World War II, US citizens gathered the pods containing this fluffy material for use as a buoyant filler for life vests that could keep a stranded soldier afloat for about 10 hours.

SPOTTED JEWELWEED
Impatiens capensis
Touch-me-not family (Balsaminaceae)
Quick ID: alternate oval coarsely toothed leaves, orange flowers with reddish spots tubular with spur

Height: 2–5' Bloom Season: July–September

Spotted jewelweed can be found in dense stands along the banks of mountain streams and in moist areas in Shenandoah. The stems contain a clear juice that was used by early settlers to apply to itchy poison ivy rashes. This plant has no problem disseminating its seeds, as the slightest touch from hummingbirds, butterflies, or other insects will cause the mature seedpods to fling their seeds up to 5 feet away—thus the common name orange touch-me-not. Hybridization sometimes occurs with the related yellow flowers of pale touch-me-not (*I. pallida*).

BUTTERFLY WEED
Asclepias tuberosa
Dogbane family (Apocynaceae)
Quick ID: alternate pointed leaves, bright orange clustered flowers, seedpods with seeds and attached tufts of white hairs

Height: 1–2' Bloom Season: June–August

The outrageously ornate orange flowers of butterfly weed are eye-catchers not only for humans but also for insects such as the monarch butterfly that pollinates this plant. The genus name *Asclepias* honors the mythological Greek god of medicine, Asclepius, whose snake-entwined staff is still a symbol of the medical profession today. Appropriately, butterfly weed was used medicinally by American Indians for rheumatism, intestinal pains, diarrhea, and heart trouble. It was most often used as a treatment for pleurisy and is therefore sometimes called "pleurisy root." They also used a poultice of bruised leaves to bind snakebites, and the stems were used to make belts.

Pale touch-me-not

WILD BERGAMOT
Monarda fistulosa
Mint family (Lamiaceae)
Quick ID: opposite leaves with tapered tip, tubular lavender flowers, reddish hairy stem

Height: 1.5–4' Bloom Season: July–August

Members of the mint family, such as wild bergamot, have leaves that are oppositely attached to a single square stem. A highly fragrant plant, it attracts many pollinators, including bees, butterflies, and ruby-throated hummingbirds. It was used by American Indians to calm colicky babies and provide a restful sleep. It was also used medicinally for flu, measles, and nosebleeds. In the 1950s a local scientist, Lena Artz, was one of the botanists who studied the varieties of wild bergamot. An unsung hero of early female scientists, she was instrumental in the research of desert-like shale barrens on Shenandoah Valley's Massanutten Mountain.

TURK'S CAP LILY
Lilium superbum
Lily family (Liliaceae)
Quick ID: several large orange drooping flowers with spotted reddish-brown recurved petals, tall stem, lance-shaped leaves in whorls

Height: 3–7' Bloom Season: July–August

Lilies are large and easily recognized by their tall stature and characteristic orange drooping flowers. The recurved petals of Turk's cap lily help to identify this native wildflower. The flower's similarity to a colorful traditional Turkish felt hat with recurved brim and pointed top led to the common name. Large butterflies such as swallowtails pollinate these lilies. The long stamens powder the butterflies' wings with pollen—you can sometimes see the rich brown dust coating the wings. In return for a nectar treat, the butterflies unknowingly transfer the pollen to the next flower. Three other large orange lilies can be found in the park, but they are favored by grazing deer and therefore infrequently found.

183

FLY POISON

Amianthium muscitoxicum

Bunchflower family (Melanthiaceae)

Quick ID: tall spikes of white to green flowers, narrow strap-like leaves that arch downward

Height: 2–3' Bloom Season: June–July

Not only is fly poison the lone member in its genus, but it has recently been moved from the lily family to the bunchflower family. It should find appropriate relatives here, as many of these plants are as toxic as fly poison. The entire plant contains alkaloid neurotoxins that cause birth defects, tremors, and even death in livestock that eat the plant. It was sometimes called "stagger grass" due to the staggering gait of affected livestock. Early colonists mashed the bulb with molasses or honey as a poison for flies. The white bottlebrush flowers are pollinated by beetles and afterward turn green. Along with fly poison, the narrower white flowers of devil's bit (*Chamaelirium luteum*) are found in Big Meadows.

FALSE HELLEBORE

Veratrum viride

Bunchflower family (Melanthiaceae)

Quick ID: alternate pleated 6- to 12-inch long leaves, yellowish-green flowers

Height: 2–8' Bloom Season: May–July

False hellebore is also known as green false hellebore, green corn lily, or Indian poke. This tall plant is found in shaded wet seepage areas in Shenandoah. All parts of this plant are poisonous and contain alkaloids that cause nausea, vomiting, irregular or slow heartbeat, and diarrhea. In the mid-1800s, false hellebore was used by physicians to treat typhoid fever, yellow fever, and pneumonia. It was also used as a sedative and to treat high blood pressure. An insecticide was made from the roots.

LARGE-FLOWERED TRILLIUM
Trillium grandiflorum
Trillium family (Trilliaceae)
Quick ID: white flowers, egg-shaped leaves with pointed tips, leaves and flowers in whorls of three

Height: 8–18" Bloom Season: April–May

A distinctive and beloved wildflower, the large-flowered trillium represents the Shenandoah National Park Association as its floral logo. Native to eastern North America, trilliums sometimes form large woodland colonies. As they age, they turn pink before wilting. In a symbiotic relationship, the seeds are dispersed by ants enticed by a glob of nutritious food attached to the seed called an elaiosome. Red trillium (*T. erectum*) is also infrequently found in the park.

CANADA VIOLET
Viola canadensis
Violet family (Violaceae)

Quick ID: five white petals with yellow center, violet streaks (nectar guide) on three bottom petals, back of petals tinged with violet, heart-shaped leaves

Height: 8–16" Bloom Season: April–July

The lovely violets of spring have challenged taxonomists with their identification and classification because some species are quite variable and they readily form hybrids. Violets such as Canada violet are white, but others are yellow, blue, or green. All violets have five petals with two at the top, two at the side, and one striped petal at the bottom. Typically striped, the lower petal acts as a landing pad for bees and other insects. The stripes, which are known as nectar guides, help guide the pollinators into the nectar source. Violets either have the leaves and flowers coming from the stem like Canada violet, or the flower stalk and leaves come directly out of the ground. Violet leaves are heart shaped, lance shaped, or finely divided.

Pink lady's slipper

YELLOW LADY'S SLIPPER
Cypripedium parviflorum
Orchid family (Orchidaceae)
Quick ID: large yellow pouched flower with lateral petals that are long, narrow, and spiral down; alternate leaves 6 to 8 inches long with noticeable lengthwise veins

Height: 8–24" Bloom Season: April–June

Orchids grown in greenhouses represent a fraction of the tens of thousands of species that grow in the wild. The vanilla bean that flavors ice cream and baked goods is the seedpod of an orchid. Lady's slipper orchids are some of the nearly thirty species of orchids native to Shenandoah. These orchids have a balloon-like pouch that resembles a bedroom slipper or moccasin. The large yellow lady's slippers (*C. parviflorum var. pubescens*) are found in rich woods, while the less common small variety (*C. parviflorum var. parviflorum*) grow in moist areas. Pink lady's slippers (*C. acaule*) are most frequent in the southern section of the park.

SHOWY ORCHIS
Galearis spectabilis
Orchid family (Orchidaceae)
Quick ID: 2 large 4- to 8-inch glossy oval leaves, 2 to 15 white and pinkish flowers

Height: 4–8" Bloom Season: April–June

Spring wildflowers are always a treat for hikers along trails in Shenandoah, but the pastel-pink blooms of showy orchis are certainly one of the most delightful surprises. Showy orchis is native to eastern and central North America and is a member of one of the largest families of flowering plants in the world with up to 35,000 species known worldwide. The three pink-to-lavender sepals converge with two lateral petals to form a hood that covers the white lower petal. Recently changed from *Orchis spectabilis*, the current genus name *Galearis* is derived from the Latin word *galea*, which means "helmet," and the species name *spectabilis*, which is Latin for "showy."

WILD COLUMBINE
Aquilegia canadensis
Buttercup family (Ranunculaceae)
Quick ID: nodding red and yellow flowers with 5 upward spurs, long slender stems, 3-lobed leaflets

Height: 1–3' Bloom Season: April–September

Blooming spring through summer on brightly lit rocky, wooded, or open slopes is an eye-catching red and yellow flower. The spectacular nodding flower has five red, backward-pointing, spur-like petals with yellow borders. The tips of the pointed spurs contain nectar. Probing for the sweet treat, hummingbirds inadvertently pollinate the flower. The genus name *Aquilegia* comes from the Latin word *aquila*, which refers to an eagle. The flower spurs imaginatively resemble an eagle's talons. Columbine comes from the Latin word *columba*, which means "dove," referring to the flower spurs that resemble the heads of circling doves.

BLACK COHOSH
Actaea racemosa
Buttercup family (Ranunculaceae)
Quick ID: white flower spikes about 12 inches long, tall pliable stems, leaves coarsely toothed with 3 leaflets

Height: 3–8' Bloom Season: June–September

The feathery white flower spikes of black cohosh wave atop tall stems that are about 3 feet tall and resemble torches or "fairy candles," as they are sometimes called. *Cohosh* is a American Indian word that means "rough" in reference to the appearance of the plants' black rhizomes (roots). Another common name, bugbane, is derived from its use as an insect repellent, and it is also used medicinally for menopausal symptoms. Like many other native plants used medicinally, black cohosh is fast disappearing from its natural habitat due to plant poaching, which is unfortunate because it is the larval food plant for the Appalachian azure butterfly. Members of this genus have recently been transferred from *Cimicifuga* to *Actaea*.

ALLEGHENY STONECROP
Hylotelephium telephioides
Stonecrop family (Crassulaceae)
Quick ID: pale pink starry flowers, succulent rounded leaves

Height: 6–12" Bloom Season: August–September

With perhaps some of the best resident views in the park, Allegheny stonecrop is happiest growing on rocky ledges and cliffs overlooking the forests below. This drought-tolerant succulent is sometimes called "live-forever," as it fades away each winter but comes back each spring. Please be careful where you put your feet when hiking on rocky areas where this and other plants may be damaged.

BLUETS
Houstonia caerulea
Madder family (Rubiaceae)
Quick ID: 4 tiny sky-blue petals with yellow center, thin wiry stem, basal spatula-shaped leaves near the ground

Height: 2–8" Bloom Season: April–July

In spring the bleak brown woodlands are awash in the sky-blue flowers of bluets. These masses of tiny flowers are sometimes called Quaker ladies because they are thought to resemble a group of bonneted women at a church meeting. The yellow centers of the flowers serve to guide tiny insects such as flies, bees, and small wasps to the pollen. The genus *Houstonia* was named to honor Dr. William Houston, a British botanist who researched and collected tropical plants.

COMMON MULLEIN
Verbascum thapsus
Figwort family (Scrophulariaceae)
Quick ID: rosette of large woolly leaves, yellow 5-petaled flowers on a tall spike

Height: 2–8' Bloom Season: June–September

In the mid-1700s, common mullein was introduced into Virginia and was used by colonists and American Indians as a fish paralyzer for easy collecting. Native to Europe, northern Africa, and Asia, the seeds of common mullein contain rotenone, which poisons fish and insects and is used as an organic pesticide dust for vegetable crops. Scientists are currently studying the correlation between the use of rotenone and Parkinson's disease. Early settlers used the large woolly leaves as warm padding for shoes and were warmed and applied to the feet for gout. It was also used as a remedy for diarrhea and hemorrhoids. The flowers were made into a tea for use as a sleep aid and to calm infants.

HIGHLAND RUSH
Juncus trifidus
Rush family (Juncaceae)
Quick ID: grass-like, branched, tiny seeds

Length: 2–11.5"

Highland rush is a plant more at home in boreal plant communities in Canada. The only spot it is found in Virginia is on one of Shenandoah's highest peaks. This overlooked plant relies on the cold, high-altitude, rocky outcrops in Shenandoah for its very existence, so watch extra carefully where you tread.

BOTTLEBRUSH GRASS
Elymus hystrix
Grass family (Poaceae)
Quick ID: bristle-tipped seeds resembling a bottlebrush

Height: 23–47"

With over 10,000 species, the grass family (Poaceae) is the fifth-largest family of plants. Grasses are an incredibly important source of nutrition for grazing animals. There are many species of grasses in Shenandoah, but the bottlebrush grass is one of the most distinctive, as the bristle-tipped seeds resemble a baby's bottlebrush.

Quick ID for Grasses, Sedges, and Rushes

	Family	Stem
Grasses	Poaceae	Jointed, usually round
Sedges	Cyperaceae	Lacking joints, usually triangular
Rushes	Juncaceae	Lacking joints, rounded and solid

Field horsetail strobili

FIELD HORSETAIL
Equisetum arvense
Horsetail family (Equisetaceae)
Quick ID: variable, some stems with whorled branches, some producing a terminal spore-bearing cone-like structure (strobilus)

Height: 6–18"

Horsetails are so named because they somewhat resemble the stiff tail of a horse. The stems contain silica and have long been used to scour and polish tools, dishes, and pans. One of the most primitive plants, during the Carboniferous Period, horsetails grew to the size of a tree. Today their decomposed remains have become the world's supply of coal, oil, and gas. American Indians used the plant as a diuretic tea to stimulate the kidneys, and it was used as a cough medicine for horses.

COMMON GROUND PINE
Dendrolycopodium obscurum
Clubmoss family (Lycopodiaceae)
Quick ID: evergreen, flattened branches with tiny, flat, sharp-pointed leaves about 0.25 inch long

Height: 1–8"

During the Devonian Period, about 400 million years ago, club mosses were one of the dominant plants of the forests—some reaching up to 100 feet tall. Today the remnants of this powerful family of plants are small plants only about ankle high. Along with horsetails, whisk ferns, and quillworts, clubmosses form a group of plants known as fern allies. The primary difference between ferns and fern allies is the presence of large, complex leaves found in the ferns. Fern allies have small, simple leaves or leaf-like structures.

SHINING CLUBMOSS
Huperzia lucidula
Clubmoss family (Lycopodiaceae)
Quick ID: evergreen, branching upright stems, tiny narrow lance-shaped shiny green leaves 0.24 to 0.6 inch long

Height: 2–6"

Seen by hikers in moist forests, the bright green spikes of shining clubmoss, or shining firmoss, grow in small tufts and spread by branching underground roots called rhizomes. The genus has been recently changed from *Lycopodium* to *Huperzia*. The genus name *Huperzia* honors Johann Peter Huperz (1771–1816), a German fern botanist, and the species name *lucidula* is from the Latin word for "shining" in reference to the plant's bright green color. When it was discovered that the dried spores found at the leaf bases were explosive, they were gathered and used by early photographers to produce a bright flash.

RATTLESNAKE FERN
Botrypus virginianus
Adder's-tongue family (Ophioglossaceae)
Quick ID: lacy triangular leaves divided into 3 parts, long single stem, fertile spike with bead-shaped spore cases

Height: 8–30"

Found throughout the park along trails in rich woodlands, rattlesnake fern has lacy, triangular, three-parted leaves that sit atop a single stalk. The fertile spike has bead-shaped spore cases that rattle when dry—not unlike the sound of a rattlesnake. American Indians boiled the roots of rattlesnake fern to make a poultice and used it for victims of snakebite. It is also known as common grape fern for the tiny, grape-like, green spore cases. Similar ferns also found in the park are cut-leaf grape fern (*Sceptridium dissectum*), bluntlobe grape fern (*S. oneidense*), and southern grape fern (*S. biternatum*).

LEATHERY GRAPE FERN
Sceptridium multifidum
Adder's-tongue family (Ophioglossaceae)
Quick ID: leathery dissected triangular leaves, spores on separate stalk

Height: 3–12"

Along with horsetails, whisk ferns, and adder's-tongue ferns, grape ferns belong to a group of plants called fern allies, which are more primitive than true ferns. Leathery grape fern is a northern plant that grows in Shenandoah's Big Meadows. New fronds appear late in the year, July through September, and the spore-bearing stalk is evident.

INTERRUPTED FERN
Osmunda claytoniana
Royal Fern family (Osmundaceae)
Quick ID: leaves blunt ended, leaflets with rounded lobes, spores on fertile leaflets about one-third up stalk

Height: 2–4'

The broad fertile fronds of interrupted fern bear spores on small brown leaflets about one-third the way up the stalk, "interrupting" the flowing lines of the frond. These special leaflets are light brown when mature. Also forming sterile fronds that are not interrupted, this fern can resemble the closely related cinnamon fern (*O. cinnamomea*), which bears its spores on a separate spike that resembles a cinnamon stick. Both of these ferns are deciduous and turn yellow in fall. The Latin species name *claytoniana* honors John Clayton (1686–1773), who made many important botanical discoveries in the New World. A large colony of interrupted ferns can be seen along Skyline Drive at milepost 37.

EBONY SPLEENWORT
Asplenium platyneuron
Spleenwort family (Aspleniaceae)
Quick ID: single leaves taper at top and bottom, leaflets eared at base with toothed edges, stem shiny black

Height: 6–15"

Ebony spleenwort is a small plant with single fronds. About eighteen ladder-like leaflets are held on distinctive wiry black stems. Ebony spleenwort can be found in shaded woods and tends to grow on rocky soils and along rocky banks and cliffs. Spleenworts were traditionally used to treat disorders of the spleen.

HAYSCENTED FERN
Dennstaedtia punctilobula
Bracken Fern family (Dennstaedtiaceae)
Quick ID: lacy yellowish-green narrow-triangular deciduous fronds covered with glandular hairs; the single unclustered fronds often grow in large colonies

Height: 1–2'

Hayscented fern forms spreading colonies along many trails in the park, sometimes filling clearings and open areas at overlooks along Skyline Drive. When gently rubbed between your fingers, the fronds smell like newly mown hay. The family name, Dennstaedtiaceae, honors August Wilhelm Dennstaedt (1776–1826), who was a German botanist.

BRACKEN FERN
Pteridium aquilinum
Bracken Fern family (Dennstaedtiaceae)
Quick ID: large, long arching stem; leaves at end divided into 3 triangular parts

Height: 2–6'

Known worldwide, bracken fern can be found on every continent except Antarctica. These ancient fern fronds have been found in the fossil record from over fifty-five million years ago. This fern does not grow in clusters as many ferns do, but is on individual upright stems and forms large colonies.

MARGINAL WOOD FERN
Dryopteris marginalis
Wood Fern family (Dryopteridaceae)

Quick ID: evergreen, leaflets longest toward middle of leaf, round sori (spore-bearing structures) at leaflet margins underneath

Height: 1–2'

The evergreen fronds of marginal wood fern, or marginal shield fern, can be found along woodland trails throughout Shenandoah. The spores of typical ferns are borne under the leaflets in dot-like structures called sori. A covering called an indusium may protect the sori. The marginal wood fern is named for its sori, which are found on the margin of each leaflet.

CHRISTMAS FERN
Polystichum acrostichoides
Wood Fern family (Dryopteridaceae)
Quick ID: evergreen, lance-shaped tapering fronds, leaflets eared at base

Height: 1–3'

One of the easiest ferns to identify, Christmas fern has leaflets that are eared at the base, forming tiny boots that resemble Christmas stockings. It is a very common fern and can be found along most trails throughout the park. The shiny, leathery fronds grow in bouquet-like circular clusters from a central rootstock.

APPALACHIAN ROCK POLYPODY
Polypodium appalachianum
Polypody family (Polypodiaceae)
Quick ID: evergreen, lance-shaped fronds widest near base, waxy leaflets begin about a third of the way up the stem, leaf tips relatively pointed

Height: 6–12"

The genus name *Polypodium* is Greek for "many footed" and refers to the marks, or "footprints," left on the rootstock when the stalks break off. The roots of polypody ferns were used medicinally by early herbalists to treat joint pain. Most of the eleven North American species of polypody ferns favor rocky slope and cliff habitats. Long thought to be the same species as rock polypody (*P. virginianum*), Appalachian rock polypody is now recognized as a separate species. Although similar in form, microscopic and genetic studies helped solve the identification mystery.

MAIDENHAIR FERN
Adiantum pedatum
Maidenhair Fern family (Pteridaceae)
Quick ID: fan-shaped frond with lacy overlapping leaves, black thin shiny stalk

Height: 1–2.5'

Maidenhair fern is an elegant native fern found in moist, rich woods in the park. The delicate, lacy leaves form a fan-shaped frond that is borne atop a thin, black, polished stalk. The genus name *Adiantum* is from a Greek word meaning "unwetted" in reference to the ability of the fronds to quickly shed water. The common name maidenhair comes from the fine hairs on its roots. It was used by early herbalists as a remedy for hair loss.

PINCUSHION MOSS
Leucobryum glaucum
White Moss family
(Leucobryaceae)
Quick ID: dense rounded
cushions or mats, light
whitish-green

Not all mosses grow on the
north side of trees as told in
fables; most mosses grow
on the dampest area of trees
regardless of the compass
orientation. Pincushion moss
is also called white cushion
moss or *leucobryum* moss.
Leucobryum means "white
moss"; this plant is so called because the leaves have a whitish cast that may help reflect light and allow
it to live in drier areas. Look for pincushion moss growing along trails such as the accessible Limberlost
Trail. Due to their highly absorbent properties, mosses were traditionally used as diapers and for feminine
hygiene. During the Civil War, mosses were also used as an absorbent dressing for soldiers' wounds.

HAIRCAP MOSS
Polytrichum commune
Haircap and Smoothcap Moss family
(Polytrichaceae)
Quick ID: wiry stalks with pointed lance-shaped
leaves arranged in a spiral

Found in most regions of the world, haircap
moss is one of the most common of the about
15,000 species of mosses in the world. Mosses
do not have flowers or seeds. Periodically they
produce thin stalks capped by spore capsules.
When the capsules dry, they crack open and
release spores that are scattered on the breeze
to germinate new mosses. Along with mosses,
liverworts and hornworts are two other groups
of plants that typically lack vascular tissue
and rely on absorption of water and nutrients
through osmosis and diffusion. Haircap mosses
have been used for thousands of years as teas;
to dissolve gallbladder and kidney stones; and
to make brooms, brushes, baskets, and rugs.

SULPHUR DUST LICHEN
Chrysothrix chlorina
Dust Lichen family (Chrysothricaceae)
Quick ID: yellow dust-like particles on rock

Type: crustose (flat)

Usually found on shaded rocks, the brilliant yellow sulphur dust lichen grows on high-altitude basic metamorphic rocks such as those on Hawksbill. This lichen indicates a very rare association of boulder lichens restricted to Shenandoah National Park. Recent studies have shown that the unique high-elevation outcrops in the park harbor lichens that are typically found growing in more northern, boreal locations. Please be aware that your footsteps can damage these unique organisms that may be many hundreds of years old.

POWDER FOOT BRITISH SOLDIER LICHEN
Cladonia incrassata
Cup and Reindeer Lichen family (Cladoniaceae)
Quick ID: greenish-gray stalk, bright red caps

Type: fruticose (shrubby)

It isn't until you sit down for a rest along the trail that the tiny red specs call your attention to the British soldier lichens growing on logs, old wooden fences, or mossy soil. The bright red "caps" that resemble the red hats worn by the British army during the Revolutionary War are actually the fruiting structure of the lichen.

THORN REINDEER LICHEN
Cladonia uncialis
Cup and Reindeer Lichen family
(Cladoniaceae)
Quick ID: grayish-green mounds, intricate branches with forked spiky tips

Type: fruticose (shrubby)

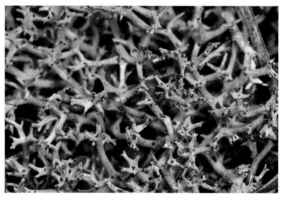

The thorn reindeer lichen grows on mossy soil mounds, stretching its tiny forked branches upward toward the sun. Brittle and spiky when dry, it becomes soft to the touch when moist. Lichens are a symbiotic relationship of two different organisms: a fungus and an alga or cyanobacterium. Also growing in the arctic, this and two other reindeer lichens are the preferred foods of arctic caribou. Reindeer and caribou are the same species of deer (*Rangifer tarandus*), but they are known as caribou in North America and reindeer in Europe, where they tend to be smaller and domesticated.

MEALY PIXIE CUP
Cladonia chlorophaea
Cup and Reindeer Lichen family (Cladoniaceae)
Quick ID: funnel-shaped, greenish-gray dots

Type: fruticose (shrubby)

These tiny lichens are fodder for the imagination, resembling tiny trumpets, funnels, or golf tees. Lichens are categorized into three main types: fruticose lichens, which are shrubby or bushy; crustose lichens, which lie flat on rocks, trees, or other substrates; and foliose lichens, which are leaf-like.

ROCK GREENSHIELD
Flavoparmelia baltimorensis
Beard and Tree Lichen family (Parmeliaceae)
Quick ID: pale green lobes, dark underneath, grows on rocks

Type: foliose (leafy)

Lichens are two organisms, a fungus and an alga, that live in a mutualistic relationship. Mutualism is a type of symbiosis in which both organisms benefit from the association. The fungus provides a home, and the alga provides the food for both of them. There are over 14,000 species of lichens in the world with about 3,600 species found in North America. Lichens grow on the ground, on rocks, and on trees. The rock greenshield grows on rocks, but similar relatives grow on trees. Lichens absorb nutrients, water, and other chemicals from the air, and are therefore good indicators of air pollution.

HALE'S ROCK BEARD LICHEN
Usnea halei
Beard and Tree Lichen family
(Parmeliaceae)
Quick ID: long pale yellowish-green
strands, gray when dry

Type: fruticose (shrubby)

Unlike most beard lichens that grow on
trees, Hale's rock beard lichen grows
on rocks. It was named to honor the
Smithsonian Institute lichenologist Mason
Hale (1928–1990), who popularized lichens
and made many important discoveries and
advances in the field. Usnic acid in beard
lichens shows promise as an antibacterial
agent in the treatment of wounds and
burns. It is sometimes used in underarm
deodorants.

GOLDEN MOON GLOW LICHEN
Dimelaena oreina
Rosette Lichen family (Physciaceae)
Quick ID: light greenish-yellow rosettes with black underneath

Type: crustose (flat)

Golden moon glow lichen is a widespread lichen that grows on sunny, exposed rocks. The yellowish
rosette of raised bumps is outlined in black, creating a moonlike pattern.

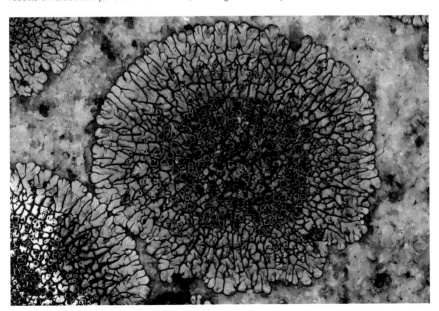

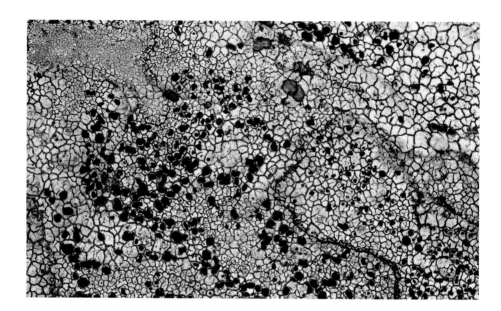

TILE LICHEN
Lecidea tessellata
Tile Lichen family (Lecideaceae)
Quick ID: grayish "tiles" with blackish "moles"

Type: crustose (flat)

There are several types of tile lichens that look as if they were fit together like tiny kitchen tiles. One species of tile lichens has been widely used to date geologic events because it grows very slowly. Crustose lichens are flat and adhere tightly to their rock (or other substrate). Particular lichens grow on particular types of rocks; tile lichens are usually found on acidic rocks such as the volcanic and metamorphic rocks in the park.

COMMON TOADSKIN LICHEN
Lasallia papulosa
Rock Tripe Lichen family (Umbilicariaceae)
Quick ID: bumpy pustules, gray when dry and green when wet

Type: foliose (leafy)

Found on rocks, the common toadskin lichen often grows alongside rock tripe lichens in the park. The bumpy pimples resemble the skin of a toad, and when wet the lichen turns toad green. Both

toadskin and rock tripe lichens were used to produce purple dye for coloring cloth and basketry by early pioneers.

SMOOTH ROCK TRIPE
Umbilicaria mammulata
Rock Tripe Lichen family (Umbilicariaceae)
Quick ID: brown, flat circle with tattered edges; bumpy black underneath; attached to rocks

Type: foliose (leafy)

Rock tripe, or naval lichen, grows from a central "stalk" that is attached to the surface of a rock. The frayed edges are brittle when dry, but the lichen becomes leathery when wet. Rock tripe has been used as a survival food, and American Indians added it to soups as a thickening agent.

Giant puffball

GEM-STUDDED PUFFBALL
Lycoperdon perlatum
Agaric family (Agaricaceae)
Quick ID: white and rounded with cone-shaped spines, white stalk

The gem-studded puffball is one of the many species of puffballs that are choice edibles when young. Another edible puffball, the giant puffball (*Calvatia maxima*) can grow as large as a basketball. With their distinctive cone-shaped spines, gem-studded puffballs often grow in clusters in fields and open woodlands. The folk remedy of inhaling puffball spores to control nosebleeds is very dangerous, as fungal particles can invade lung tissues.

DESTROYING ANGEL
Amanita bisporigera
Amanita family (Amanitaceae)
Quick ID: smooth white cap, white stalk with membranous white ring (annulus), white "sac" around base (volva), white gills

The name says it all. The destroying angel mushroom is an enchantingly lovely white mushroom that is so toxic that one bite can ultimately cause death. Many members of the amanita family are poisonous. They often are white with a thin skirt around the stalk and a white sac called a volva around the base. If mistakenly eaten, the toxins do not cause symptoms right away, but later the victim experiences diarrhea and cramps. Symptoms then subside, but without a liver transplant within a week, death will follow. Do not consume any mushroom unless you are absolutely sure of its identification.

VIOLET CORAL FUNGUS
Clavaria zollingeri
Club fungi family (Clavariaceae)

Quick ID: violet forked tubular branches from 2 to 4 inches

Even through the violet coral fungus is small, it is a showstopper with its lovely violet color so unique in nature. Growing on the ground or in mosses, the dense clumps of diverging forked branches resemble colorful undersea corals. Other types of coral fungi may have more or less branching or none at all and come in a variety of colors, including orange, white, yellow, and red. The violet coral fungus and others contain proteins called lectins, which are used in chromatography tests and blood typing.

Crested coral fungus

Golden fairy club

VISCID VIOLET CORT
Cortinarius iodes
Cortinarius family (Cortinariaceae)
Quick ID: lavender with yellowish spots and streaks, slimy cap and stem

Few organisms in nature are purple, but the viscid violet cort, or webcap, has a slimy purple cap and stem and produces a reddish-rusty brown spore print. Common in eastern North America, this species has also been found in Costa Rica and Colombia. Although it is not edible, look for this mushroom in August and September, especially under oaks where it poses nicely for colorful pictures.

JACK-O'-LANTERN
Omphalotus olearius
Funnel family (Marasmiaceae)
Quick ID: orange to yellow-orange gills, margin down-curved, bioluminescent, in clusters at base of hardwood trees (especially oaks)

To novice mushroom hunters the jack-o'-lantern mushroom looks very similar to the highly prized edible chanterelle (*Cantharellus spp.*), but ingesting this mushroom causes severe illness. It's noted for its bioluminescent properties, glowing blue-green in low light. This mushroom contains an enzyme called luciferase that acts on the pigment luciferin, which causes it to glow.

FROST'S BOLETE

Boletus frostii

Bolete family (Boletaceae)

Quick ID: red sticky slimy cap, red pores, network-like pattern on stem, stains blue, exuded watery golden drops underneath the cap

If you look under the cap of a bolete, you will see tiny spongy-looking pores rather than the customary gills of a mushroom. The spores are held in these pores and released when mature. The bright red, sticky cap of Frost's bolete is quite distinctive. It can be found growing under oaks in late summer through early fall. It stains blue when injured, and its edibility is not recommended, as it can cause gastrointestinal distress.

RED SLIMY STALKED PUFFBALL

Calostoma cinnabarinum

Thick Stain Puffball family (Sclerodermataceae)

Quick ID: round ball covered in slime on a spongy red stalk

The red slimy stalked puffball looks like a cherry tomato onto which someone dropped a congealed egg white. The red color and tough gelatinous covering have led to another common name—stalked puffball-in-aspic—referring to the cold jelly-like dish called tomato aspic. These mushrooms are most common in the dry habitats of the park's southern section.

GOLDEN CHANTERELLE
Cantharellus cibarius
Chanterelle family (Cantharellaceae)
Quick ID: orange to yellowish-orange, funnel shaped, blunt ridges under cap onto stalk, grows singly in groups on ground

Loved by mycophiles (mushroom lovers), chanterelles are considered one of the most choice edibles in the culinary fungal world. Not only are they highly prized for their delightful mild fruity taste, but they are also high in potassium and vitamin C and are one of the richest natural sources of vitamin D. The similar jack-o-lantern mushroom (*Omphalotus olearius*) has sharp, forked gills and is poisonous.

GREEN STAIN FUNGUS
Chlorociboria aeruginascens
Earth Tongue family
(Helotiaceae)
Quick ID: blue-green cup fungus, green-stained wood

The saucer-shaped fruiting bodies of the green stain fungus are rarely seen, but the green-stained wood caused by the fungus is commonly seen in fallen logs throughout the park. This colorful fungus contains a pigment called xylindein that stains the wood a bluish-green color. During the fifteenth century, woodworking artisans used the stained wood to add color to decorative wooden panels.

YELLOW MOREL
Morchella esculentoides
Morel family (Morchellaceae)
Quick ID: brownish conical honeycomb or net-like ridges attached all the way down the stalk, hollow stem

The spring treasure hunt for morels begins when the oak leaves are about the size of a mouse's ear. Morel hunters carefully guard the secret places where they've found these treasures in the past. Sometimes called "merkels," the mushrooms are soaked in salt water to remove any invertebrates then cooked in butter or added to dishes such as scrambled eggs. The yellow, or common morel, is one of several species of morels found in the park. The poisonous false morel (*Gyromitra esculenta*) has a wrinkled cap that is not attached all the way down the stalk, and the stem is often cottony inside rather than hollow.

False morel

False morel

COMMON STINKHORN
Phallus impudicus
Stinkhorn family (Phallaceae)
Quick ID: foul odor, tall white column, slimy
greenish-brown cone-shaped cap

To find a stinkhorn, just follow your nose. These
fungi emit a powerful stench of rotting flesh mixed
with feces. The unusual phallic shape of these
offensive mushrooms is sometimes shocking
for innocent eyes. Arising from an egg-shaped
structure beneath the ground, the fruiting body
attracts flies and carrion beetles to carry the sticky
spores. The "egg" stage is edible. Other stinkhorns,
including the reddish pink dog stinkhorn (*Mutinus
caninus*), may be found in the park.

HEMLOCK VARNISH SHELF
Ganoderma tsugae
Ganoderma family
(Ganodermataceae)
Quick ID: shiny reddish-brown shelf
fungus with yellow then white
margins, grows on conifers (especially
hemlocks), whitish pores that bruise
brown

The beautiful reddish-brown surface
of this shelf fungus gives the
appearance that someone has spread
a coat of varnish on top—thus the common name varnish shelf. Hemlock varnish shelf is related to another
polypore called reishi, or ling chih (*G. lucidum*), which has long been used in the Orient as an herbal remedy
for many ailments and diseases. With the decline of the great hemlock forests in Shenandoah due to the
hemlock woolly adelgid infestation, this fungus may become increasingly rare.

SULPHUR SHELF
Laetiporus sulphureus
Polypore family (Polyporaceae)
Quick ID: orange brackets, yellow edges, grows on trees (especially oaks)

Commonly known as "chicken of the woods," the yellowish-orange brackets of sulphur shelf are a well-known edible that tastes a bit like chicken. The shelves can grow up to 10 inches across and are attached to trees or tree stumps. Sulphur shelves cause brown rot in trees, eventually leading to the tree's death. Although edible, in certain people ingestion can cause nausea.

TURKEY TAIL
Trametes versicolor
Polypore family (Polyporaceae)
Quick ID: concentric multicolored rings on wood, pores underneath

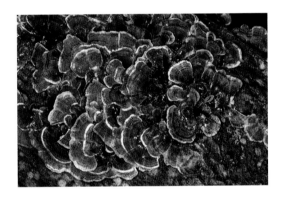

Well named for its resemblance to the tail of a turkey, this fungus is commonly seen growing on trees and fallen logs throughout Shenandoah. Turkey tail has long been used for medicinal purposes in the Orient. High in antioxidants, the immune boosting properties of turkey tail mushrooms may be useful in supporting medical treatments for breast, gastric, and colon cancers.

RED WRINKLED RUSSULA
Russula rugulosa
Russula family (Russulaceae)
Quick ID: cap red (variable), white stem, white gills

Russulas are a widespread group of mushrooms that often have red caps but which can range from yellow to green. The red wrinkled russula is named for the subtle venations on the surface of its cap. Like many species of mushrooms, russulas are mycorrhizal, which means they live in a symbiotic relationship with a tree or other plant. The fungus gets nourishment from the tree in the form of sugars, and the tree gains water from the fungus as well as essential nutrients. The North American Mycological Association (namyco .org) and local clubs sponsor mushroom forays locally and across the nation to determine the variety of fungi species and to encourage much-needed research in the field of mycology.

AZALEA GALL
Exobasidium vaccinii
Exobasidia family (Exobasidiaceae)
Quick ID: light green mass on azaleas turning velvety white then brown and hard

Galls are growths on plants caused by bacteria, viruses, fungi, or other insect pathogens. The fungus *Exobasidium vaccinii* infects azaleas, causing fleshy, swollen, irregularly shaped formations on the stem and leaves. Other members of the heath family, such as blueberries, huckleberries, mountain laurel, and rhododendron, are susceptible to gall formation.

WOOL SOWER GALL
Callirhytis seminator
Gall Wasp family (Cynipidae)
Quick ID: white spongy balls tinged with pink spots

The wool sower gall is caused by a type of small gall wasp that lays its eggs on the twigs, buds, or leaves of white oaks. Other insects that cause galls are gall midges and gall mites. This gall develops as a white ball with pinkish spots. The galls contain structures that resemble seeds where the wasps develop from grubs. The gall secretes nutrients that nourish the growing grubs. A gall that looks like a small greenish-tan apple is the very common oak apple gall (*Amphibolips confluenta*).

BLUEBERRY STEM GALL
Hemadas nubilipennis
Pteromalid Wasp family (Pteromalidae)
Quick ID: bulbose red-tinged growth, turns brown with age

A tiny black wasp causes red cherry-like galls on blueberry twigs. Look for them on the blueberry shrubs in Big Meadows. The wasp lays its eggs in the tips of stems, and the plant reacts by forming a multichambered growth of plant tissue over the mass. Sometimes other wasp species parasitize the gall and lay their eggs in with the original wasp's eggs. The young wasps emerge from the gall through tiny holes that they chew.

CEDAR-APPLE RUST
Gymnosporangium juniper-virginianae
Rust family (Pucciniaceae)
Quick ID: yellow-orange spots on apple leaves, bright orange gelatinous-armed balls on cedars

Although most people have never heard of cedar-apple rust, orchardists are very familiar with this family of rusts, which can infect their apple trees and therefore their source of income. This startling alien-like gall is most noticeable on eastern red cedars after a rain, when it expands into a bright orange, tennis ball–size, gelatinous gall with slimy tentacles. The gall requires two hosts and the spores, which can travel on the wind up to 2 miles then land on apple trees, infecting the leaves with yellow-orange spots. In spring, when conditions are right, cedar trees near the North Entrance sport these oddities of nature.

OAK APPLE GALL
Amphibolips confluenta
Gall Wasp family (Cynipidae)
Quick ID: round papery thin, golf ball size, 1- to 2-inch spheres, green turning to brown

Many insects cause oak galls, including gall wasps that lay their eggs on oak leaves and twigs. The larvae hatch and tunnel into the plant. The plant overreacts and rapidly grows thick tissue around the invader to keep it from spreading. The larvae get protection from the gall, and the plant is usually not affected. In spring, they exit the gall and fly away as adults.

GOLDENROD GALL
Eurosta solidaginis
Peacock Fly family (Tephritidae)
Quick ID: large marble size, brown on goldenrod stem

The goldenrod gall fly lays its eggs on a goldenrod, and the larva tunnel into the stem where saliva from the larva stimulates the plant to form a rounded gall that houses the larvae. When the larvae emerge as adults in spring, they only have about two weeks to breed, lay eggs on another goldenrod, and begin the cycle again. During the long winter months, the larvae inside the gall are an important source of food for animals, such as squirrels, and many birds, including chickadees and woodpeckers.

POISON IVY GALL
Aculops rhois
Gall Mite family (Eriophyidae)
Quick ID: small green to reddish patches on upper leaf

For those of us who have suffered the relentless itch caused by poison ivy, it is somewhat comforting to know that the plant has an adversary that attacks its leaves. A tiny mite known as the poison ivy gall mite attacks the upper surface of poison ivy leaves and the plant tissue reacts, forming green to reddish blisters on the leaf. This mite also attacks other related species. It is unknown whether these blisters cause any damage or discomfort to the plant, but some of us look at these galls with silent glee.

BLACK KNOT
Apiosporina morbosa
Venturia family (Venturiaceae)
Quick ID: black thick irregular swellings on branches and twigs of cherry trees

Black knot is a fungus that infects cherry and plum trees causing a thick black swollen gall on the twigs and branches. The gall cuts off the nutrient supply to the twig, and it causes death of the twig and sometimes the entire tree.

LIMESTONE

Quick ID: gray, fine grained

Type: sedimentary rock

Although little limestone is found within the boundaries of the park, it underlies the Shenandoah Valley to the west and provides the channel through which the Shenandoah River twists and winds. Limestone erodes more quickly than the resistant granites, greenstones, and quartzites of the Blue Ridge Mountains. At the Shenandoah Valley Overlook (milepost 2.8), you can see in the distance a limestone quarry just past the Cedar Creek and Belle Grove National Historic Park. Limestone was formed from the remains of marine organisms that lived in an ocean once covering this area. The many caves, caverns, and sinkholes in Virginia were formed when water dissolved the limestone. Many of the caverns are adorned with slow-growing, intricate formations such as flowstone, stalactites, and stalagmites.

SANDSTONE

Quick ID: tan, gray, or reddish; coarse grained

Type: sedimentary rock

The sandstone in Shenandoah is a type of sedimentary rock that was deposited in an ancient ocean called Iapetus that once covered this land. The rocky ledges evident along Skyline Drive next to Rocky Top Overlook (milepost 78.1) and Sawmill Ridge Overlook (milepost 95.9) are composed of sandstone.

GRANITE

Quick ID: various shades of gray, white, and black; coarse grained with scattered dark minerals

Type: igneous rock

Granite is a white or grayish igneous rock with grains of various colors. Igneous rocks are formed when magma deep below the earth's surface cools slowly and crystallizes. At Hogback Overlook (milepost 21), you can see a good example of this ancient rock type called granodiorite, which is composed of quartz and feldspar. Old Rag Mountain is formed from

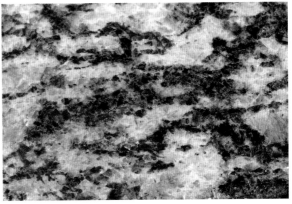

Old Rag granite

granite that is about 1.1 billion years old. Old Rag granite is composed of blue-gray minerals of glassy whitish quartz and feldspar that is generally milky white or whitish pink and forms crystals that reflect light. Dark flecks composed of pyroxene, hornblende, and biotite (a black mica) can also be seen in the granite, along with the small red dots of garnets.

GNEISS

Quick ID: light- and dark-colored discontinuous layers; coarse grained

Type: metamorphic rock

Along with granite, gneiss (pronounced "nice") is one of the oldest rock types in Shenandoah, and together they form the basement layer known as the Basement Complex (previously known as the Pedlar Formation). These ancient rocks are about 1.2 billion years old and were formed long before any terrestrial life was present on earth. Basement Complex gneiss can be seen at Little Devils Stairs Overlook (milepost 20.1), Marys Rock Tunnel (milepost 32.2), and Buck Hollow Overlook (milepost 32.9).

Columnar joints

METABASALT (GREENSTONE)

Quick ID: fine-grained, dark blackish-grayish to grayish-green

Type: metamorphic rock

Metamorphosed rocks of metabasalt underlie the mountains of Shenandoah. When the Appalachian Mountains were forming, basalt was compressed under great pressure and was metamorphosed into metabasalts or greenstones. The original basalt flows occurred about 570 million years ago, and then they were metamorphosed into greenstone during the Allegheny Orogeny 300 to 350 million years ago. You can see greenstone at Crescent Rock Overlook (mile 44.4) and Franklin Cliffs Overlook (mile 49.0). Intrusive rock formations from feeder dikes of lava flows can be seen at Little Devil Stairs (mile 19.4). At the Limberlost area (mile 43), columnar joints can be seen from an ancient lava flow that was extruded onto the surface of the earth and then cooled, forming the polygonal shaped columns.

PHYLLITE

Quick ID: greenish-gray, wavy

Type: metamorphic rock

Phyllite has a tendency to split into thin sheets of shiny rocks containing mica. The phyllites in the park were originally sediments of mud that were deposited in the bottom of ancient lagoons and volcanic ash deposits. Hensley Hollow Overlook at milepost 64.4 is a good place to see phyllite.

QUARTZITE

Quick ID: variable coloration from gray
to white

Type: metamorphic rock

Quartzite is white rock that was
formed from quartz-rich sandstone that
recrystallized under great pressure
due to continental collision. Look for
quartzite along the Bearfence Mountain
Trail (milepost 56.4). The light-colored
cliffs that you can see from Two Mile
Run Overlook (milepost 76.2), Brown
Mountain Overlook (milepost 76.9), and
Rocky Top Overlook (milepost 78.1) are

also quartzite. The rock layer underlying the quartzite is sandstone and phyllite. These types of sedimentary
rocks erode at a faster rate than quartzite, which causes the more resistant rock to fall in fragments,
creating talus slopes.

REFERENCES

Abramson, R., and J. Haskell, eds. *Encyclopedia of Appalachia*. Knoxville, TN: University of Tennessee Press, 2006.

Amberson, J. *Short Hikes in Shenandoah National Park*. Luray, VA: Shenandoah National Park Association, 2010.

Arora, D. *Mushrooms Demystified*. 2nd ed. Berkeley, CA: Ten Speed Press, 1986.

Badger, R. L. *Geology Along Skyline Drive*. Luray, VA: Shenandoah National Park Association, 2012.

Beane, J. C., A. L. Braswell, J. C. Mitchell, W. M. Palmer, and J. R. Harrison. *Amphibians & Reptiles of the Carolinas and Virginia*. 2nd ed. Chapel Hill, NC: The University of North Carolina Press, 2010.

Bell, R. B., and A. H. Lindsey. *Fall Color and Woodland Harvests*. Chapel Hill, NC: Laurel Hill Press, 1990.

Bolgiano, C. *The Appalachian Forest: A Search for Roots and Renewal*. Mechanicsburg, PA: Stackpole Books, 1998.

Brinkley, E. S. *Field Guide to Birds of North America*. New York: Sterling Publishing Co., 2008.

Brodo, I. M., S. D. Sharnoff, and S. Sharnoff. *Lichens of North America*. New Haven, CT: Yale University Press, 2001.

Brooks, M. *The Appalachians*. Boston, MA: Houghton Mifflin, 1965.

Calhoun, C. L. *Old Southern Apples*. White River Junction, VT: Chelsea Green Publishing, 2010.

Capinera, J. L., R. D. Scott, and T. J. Walker. *Field Guide to Grasshoppers, Katydids, and Crickets of the United States*. Ithaca, NY: Cornell University Press, 2004.

Cavender, A. *Folk Medicine in Southern Appalachia*. Chapel Hill, NC: The University of North Carolina Press, 2003.

Clemants, S., and C. Gracie. *Wildflowers in the Field and Forest: A Field Guide to the Northeastern United States*. New York: Oxford University Press, 2006.

Cobb, B. *A Field Guide to Ferns and Their Related Families*. New York: Houghton Mifflin, 1984.

Conant, R., and J. T. Collins. *A Field Guide to Reptiles & Amphibians: Eastern and Central North America*. 3rd ed. New York: Houghton Mifflin, 1998.

Conners, J. A. *Shenandoah National Park: An Interpretive Guide*. Blacksburg, VA: The McDonald & Woodward Publishing Company, 1988.

Dunkle, S. W. *Dragonflies Through Binoculars: A Field Guide to Dragonflies of North America.* New York: Oxford University Press, 2000.

Eaton, R. E., and K. Kaufman. *Kaufman Field Guide to Insects of North America.* New York: Houghton Mifflin, 2007.

Fleming, C., M. B. Lobstein, and B. Tufty. *Finding Wildflowers in the Washington-Baltimore Area.* Baltimore, MD: Johns Hopkins University Press, 1995.

Forsyth, A. *Mammals of North America: Temperate and Arctic Regions.* Buffalo, NY: Firefly Books, 2006.

Frick-Ruppert, J. *Mountain Nature: A Seasonal Natural History of the Southern Appalachians.* Chapel Hill, NC: The University of North Carolina Press, 2010.

Gildart, B., and J. Gildart. *Hiking Shenandoah National Park.* 4th ed. Guilford, CT: Falcon-Guides, 2012.

———. *Best Easy Day Hikes Shenandoah National Park.* 2nd ed. Guilford, CT: Falcon-Guides, 2006.

Glassberg, J. *Butterflies Through Binoculars: The East.* New York: Oxford University Press, 1999.

Harris, A. G., E. Tuttle, and S. D. Tuttle. *Geology of National Parks.* 6th ed. Dubuque, IA: Kendall/Hunt Publishing, 2004.

Heatwole, H. *Guide to Skyline Drive and Shenandoah National Park.* Luray, VA: Shenandoah Natural History Association, 1978.

Howell, P. K. *Medicinal Plants of the Southern Appalachians.* Mountain City, GA: BotanoLogos Books, 2006.

Jenkins, R. E., and N. M. Burkhead. *Freshwater Fishes of Virginia.* Bethesda, MD: American Fisheries Society, 1994.

Johnson, D. W. *A Birder's Guide to Virginia.* Colorado Springs, CO: American Birding Association, 1997.

Kirkman, L. K., C. L. Brown, and D. J. Leopold. *Native Trees of the Southeast.* Portland, OR: Timber Press, 2007.

Lambert, D. *The Undying Past of Shenandoah National Park.* Lanham, MD: The Rowman & Littlefield Publishing Group, 2001.

Lindsay, T., and P. Lindsey. *Birds of Shenandoah National Park.* Luray, VA: Shenandoah Natural History Association, 1997.

Little, E. L. *The Audubon Society Field Guide to North American Trees, Eastern Region.* New York: Chanticleer Press, 1980.

Manville, R. H. *The Mammals of Shenandoah National Park.* Luray, VA: Shenandoah Natural History Association, 1956.

Mazzeo, P. M. *Trees of Shenandoah National Park.* Luray, VA: Shenandoah Natural History Association, 1967.

Miller, J. H., and K. V. Miller. *Forest Plants of the Southeast and Their Wildlife Uses.* Rev. ed. Athens, GA: University of Georgia Press, 2005.

Milne, L., and M. Milne. *The Audubon Society Field Guide to North American Insects and Spiders.* New York: Chanticleer Press, 1980.

Page, L. M., and B. M. Burr. *Peterson Field Guide to Freshwater Fishes of North America North of Mexico.* 2nd ed. New York: Houghton Mifflin Harcourt Publishing Company, 2011.

Petrides, G. A. *A Field Guide to Trees and Shrubs.* 2nd ed. New York: Houghton Mifflin, 1986.

Roody, W. C. *Mushrooms of West Virginia and the Central Appalachians.* Lexington, KY: The University Press of Kentucky, 2003.

Sibley, D. A. *The Sibley Guide to Birds.* 2nd ed. New York: Chanticleer Press, 2014

Simpson, A., and R. Simpson. *Wildflowers of Shenandoah National Park.* Guilford, CT: FalconGuides, 2011.

Simpson, M. *Birds of the Blue Ridge Mountains.* Chapel Hill, NC: The University of North Carolina Press, 1992.

Stokes, D. W. *The Natural History of Wild Shrubs and Vines.* New York: Harper & Row, 1981.

Thieret, J. W., W. A. Niering, and N. C. Olmstead. *National Audubon Society Field Guide to North American Wildflowers, Eastern Region.* Rev. ed. New York: Alfred A. Knopf, Inc./Chanticleer Press, 2001.

Virginia Botanical Associates. 2012. *Digital Atlas of the Virginia Flora* (www.vaplantatlas .org). c/o Virginia Botanical Associates, Blacksburg, VA.

Virginia Department of Game and Inland Fisheries. *Virginia Birding and Wildlife Trail, Mountain Trail.* www.dgif.virginia.gov/vbwt.

Virginia Department of Wildlife Resources. 2022. *Virginia's Wildlife.* https://dwr.virginia .gov/wildlife/wildlife-information/.

Virginia Herpetological Society. 2022. www.virginiaherpetologicalsociety.com.

Weakley, A. S., and Southeastern Flora Team. *2022 Flora of the Southeastern United States.* University of North Herbarium, North Carolina Botanical Garden. https://ncbg .unc.edu/2022/04/26/new-edition-released-flora-of-the-southeastern-u-s.

Webster, W. D., J. F. Parnell, and W. C. Biggs. *Mammals of the Carolinas, Virginia & Maryland.* Chapel Hill, NC: The University of North Carolina Press, 1985.

Weidensaul, S. *Mountains of the Heart.* Golden, CO: Fulcrum Publishing, 1994.

Whisnant, A. M., D. E. Whisnant, and R. Silver. *Shenandoah National Park Official Handbook*. Virginia Beach, VA: Donning Company Publishers, 2011.

Wigginton, E., and his students, eds. *Foxfire 3*. New York: Anchor Books/Random House, 1975.

Wilson, D. E., and S. Ruff, eds. *The Smithsonian Book of North American Mammals*. Washington, DC: Smithsonian Institution, 1999.

Helpful Websites

Animal Diversity Web: animaldiversity.org

Cornell Lab of Ornithology: www.allaboutbirds.org

Cornell Lab of Ornithology—Merlin: merlin.allaboutbirds.org

Hawk Migration Association of North America: www.hmana.org

GLOSSARY

achene: dry, one-seeded fruits with the outer wall enclosing the seed

alkaloid: bitter compounds produced by plants to discourage predators

alternate leaves: growing singly on a stem without an opposite leaf

anther: tip of a flower's stamen that produces pollen grains

arboreal: living in trees

basal: at the base

bioluminescence: light produced by a chemical reaction within a living organism

bulb: underground structure made up of layered, fleshy scales

cache: storage area of food and other items

capsule: a dry fruit that releases seeds through splits or holes

carrion: remains of a deceased animal

catkin: a spike, either upright or drooping, of tiny flowers

commensalism: a type of symbiosis where one species benefits while a second species is neither harmed nor benefitted

compound leaf: a leaf divided into two or more leaflets

corm: rounded, solid underground stem

deciduous: a tree that seasonally loses its leaves

diurnal: active by day

drupe: outer fleshy fruit usually having a single hard pit that encloses a seed

ecosystem: a biological environment consisting of all the living organisms in a particular area as well as the nonliving components such as water, soil, air, and sunlight

endemic: growing only in a specific region or habitat

ethnobotany: the study of the relationship between plants and people

evergreen: a tree that keeps its leaves (often needles) year-round

genus: taxonomic rank below family and above species (always capitalized and italicized)

glean: to pick small insects from foliage

habitat: the area or environment where an organism lives or occurs

host: an organism that harbors another organism

introduced: referring to a species living outside its native range; often introduced by human activity

leaflet: a part of a compound leaf; may resemble an entire leaf but is borne on a vein of a leaf rather than the stem. Leaflets are referred to as pinnae; compound leaves are pinnate (featherlike).

local resident: nonmigratory species found year-round in an area; also "resident"

marsupial: class of mammals that carry young in a pouch

metamorphic rock: a rock that has been altered by extreme heat and pressure, such as gneiss, schist, or quartzite

migration: movement of birds and other animals between breeding grounds and wintering areas

mutualism: a type of symbiosis where both organisms benefit

mycorrhiza (pl. mycorrhizae): the symbiotic, mutually beneficial relationship between a fungus and the roots of a plant

nape: area at the back of the head

native: a species indigenous or endemic to an area

nectar: sweet liquid produced by flowers to attract pollinators

niche: an organism's response to available resources and competitors (like a human's job)

nocturnal: active at night

omnivore: an organism that feeds on a variety of foods, including both plant and animal materials

opposite leaves: growing in pairs along the stem

parasitism: where one organism benefits at the expense of another organism

pollen: small powdery particles that contain the plant's male sex cells

pollination: transfer of pollen from an anther (male) to a stigma (female)

refugia: relict population

rhizome: underground stem that grows horizontally and sends up shoots

rufous: reddish-brown coloration

sepal: usually green leaf-like structures found underneath the flower

species: taxonomic rank below genus (always italicized but never capitalized); also called "specific epithet"

stamen: male part of the flower composed of a filament, or stalk, and anther, the sac at the tip of the filament that produces pollen

symbiosis: association of unlike organisms that benefits one or both

taxonomy: study of scientific classifications

toothed: jagged or serrated edge

torpor: short-term state of decreased physiological activity, including reduced body temperature and metabolic rate

wing bar: line of contrastingly colored plumage formed by the tips of the flight feathers of birds

winged: thin, flattened expansion on the sides of a plant part

INDEX

ABOUT THE AUTHORS

As professional photographers, biologists, and authors, Ann and Rob Simpson are noted national park experts, having spent years involved with research and interpretation in US national parks. They have written numerous books on national parks from coast to coast that promote wise and proper use of natural habitats and environmental stewardship. As a former chief of interpretation and national park board member, Rob has a unique understanding of the inner workings of the national park system. In cooperation with American Park Network, both have led Canon "Photography in the Parks" workshops in major national parks, including Grand

Canyon, Yellowstone, Yosemite, and Great Smoky Mountains.

Ann teaches biology at Laurel Ridge Community College in Middletown, Virginia. Rob is retired from teaching natural resources at the college. The Simpsons regularly lead international photo tours to parks and natural history destinations around the world. They are members of the following professional organizations: Outdoor Writers Association of America (OWAA), Virginia Outdoor Writers Association (VOWA), Mason-Dixon Outdoor Writers Association (M-DOWA), North American Nature Photography Association (NANPA), and Virginia Native Plant Society (VNPS).

Long known for their stunning images of the natural world, their work has been widely published in magazines such as *National Geographic, Time, National Wildlife*, and *Ranger Rick* as well as many calendars, postcards, and books. You can see their work at Simpsons' Nature Photography (www.agpix.com/snphotos).